Bob Dylan's New York

JUNE SKINNER SAWYERS

THE
History
PRESS

Published by The History Press
Charleston, SC
www.historypress.com

Front cover: courtesy PBS/Photofest.

Unless otherwise noted, all images are by the author or from the author's collection.
Maps designed by Kim Rusch.

First published 2022

Manufactured in the United States

ISBN 9781467149662

Library of Congress Control Number: 2021949182

Notice: The information in this book is true and complete to the best of our knowledge. It is offered without guarantee on the part of the author or The History Press. The author and The History Press disclaim all liability in connection with the use of this book.

CONTENTS

ACKNOWLEDGEMENTS

This book is built on the scholarship of many other people. Especially helpful were the works of Greil Marcus, Sean Wilentz, Michael Gray and Christopher Ricks, as well as Dylan biographies by Howard Sounes, Robert Shelton and Bob Spitz, among others. Memoirs describing New York in the 1950s, 1960s and 1970s were also helpful. Most gratifying of all was the time I spent walking up and down the streets of Manhattan, from Greenwich Village to the Upper West Side. I also visited the singer's home state of Minnesota, where I had the pleasure of attending a Dylan conference in Minneapolis and met such important Dylan scholars as Michael Gray and Stephen Scobie, stomped his old Dinkytown haunts and took a bus tour to Hibbing, in the heart of the Mesabi Iron Range (and where I had a lovely meal at the much-missed Zimmy's restaurant). I would like to take this opportunity to thank numerous people for their invaluable assistance and input over the years, including Theresa Albini, Colleen Sheehy, Marco Matonich, Robert Dunn, Mitch Blank, Tiffany Collanino of the Woody Guthrie Archives, Ronald Cohen and Jonathan Smele. Special recognition goes to Anthony DeCurtis, Villager and Dylan scholar, for his insights. Thank you to Deirdre Greene and Nigel Quinney, my original publishers, for taking on this project and bringing it to fruition, and to Banks Smither and Rick Delaney at The History Press, for helping me put this revised edition together.

greenwich village

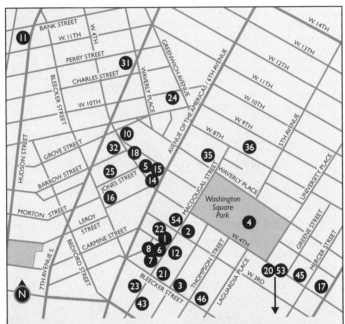

- ❶ Café Wha?: 115 MacDougal St.
- ❷ Café Bizarre: 106 West Third St.*
- ❸ Mills House and Village Gate: 158 Bleecker St.*
- ❹ Washington Square Park: foot of Fifth Ave.
- ❺ Allan Block Sandal Shop: 171 West Fourth St.*
- ❻ Gaslight Café: 116 MacDougal St.*
- ❼ Kettle of Fish: 114 MacDougal St.*
- ❽ The Commons/Fat Black Pussycat: 105 MacDougal St.*
- ❿ One Sheridan Square
- ⓫ White Horse Tavern: 567 Hudson St.
- ⓬ Folklore Center: 110 MacDougal St.*
- ⓮ 161 West Fourth St.
- ⓯ Music Inn: 169 West Fourth St.
- ⓰ Zito's Bakery: 259 Bleecker St.*
- ⓱ Gerde's Folk City: 11 West Fourth St.*
- ⓲ Newspaper kiosk: Sheridan Square
- ⓴ Supreme Court Building: 111 Centre St.

- ㉑ Café Figaro: 184 Bleecker St.*
- ㉒ Caffe Reggio: 119 MacDougal St.
- ㉓ Caffe Dante: 79–81 MacDougal St.
- ㉔ Almanac House: 130 West Tenth St.
- ㉕ Jones St. between Bleecker St. and West Fourth St.
- ㉛ Village Vanguard: 178 Seventh Ave.
- ㉜ Sheridan Square Playhouse: 99 Seventh Ave.*
- ㉟ Hotel Earle: 103 Waverly Place*
- ㊱ Eighth St. Bookshop: 17 and 32 West Eighth St.*
- ㊸ 94 MacDougal St.
- ㊺ Bottom Line: 15 West Fourth St.*
- ㊻ The Other End*/The Bitter End: 147 Bleecker St.
- ㊾ Housing Works Bookstore Café: 126 Crosby St.
- ㊴ Groove: 125 MacDougal St.

* Indicates that this is the former location of the site, which has now closed or moved.

upper west side, upper east side; and midtown

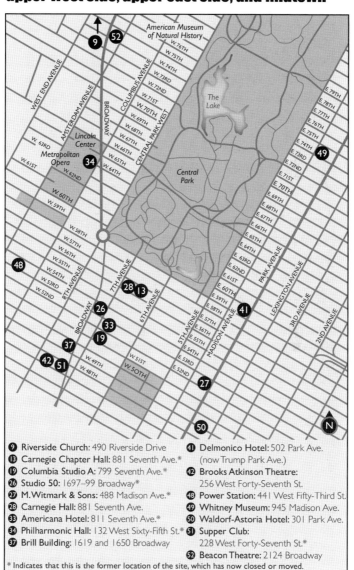

9 **Riverside Church:** 490 Riverside Drive

13 **Carnegie Chapter Hall:** 881 Seventh Ave.*

19 **Columbia Studio A:** 799 Seventh Ave.*

26 **Studio 50:** 1697–99 Broadway*

27 **M. Witmark & Sons:** 488 Madison Ave.*

28 **Carnegie Hall:** 881 Seventh Ave.

33 **Americana Hotel:** 811 Seventh Ave.*

34 **Philharmonic Hall:** 132 West Sixty-Fifth St.*

37 **Brill Building:** 1619 and 1650 Broadway

41 **Delmonico Hotel:** 502 Park Ave.
(now Trump Park Ave.)

42 **Brooks Atkinson Theatre:**
256 West Forty-Seventh St.

48 **Power Station:** 441 West Fifty-Third St.

49 **Whitney Museum:** 945 Madison Ave.

50 **Waldorf-Astoria Hotel:** 301 Park Ave.

51 **Supper Club:**
228 West Forty-Seventh St.*

52 **Beacon Theatre:** 2124 Broadway

* Indicates that this is the former location of the site, which has now closed or moved.

midtown; chelsea; and gramercy park

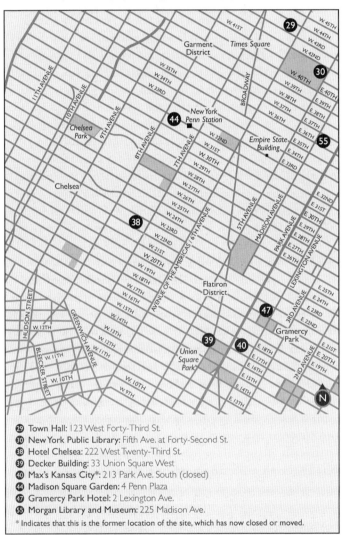

29 **Town Hall:** 123 West Forty-Third St.
30 **New York Public Library:** Fifth Ave. at Forty-Second St.
38 **Hotel Chelsea:** 222 West Twenty-Third St.
39 **Decker Building:** 33 Union Square West
40 **Max's Kansas City*:** 213 Park Ave. South (closed)
44 **Madison Square Garden:** 4 Penn Plaza
47 **Gramercy Park Hotel:** 2 Lexington Ave.
55 **Morgan Library and Museum:** 225 Madison Ave.

* Indicates that this is the former location of the site, which has now closed or moved.

INTRODUCTION

BOB DYLAN'S NEW YORK DREAM

If I had to do it all over again, I'd be a schoolteacher…
—Bob Dylan

In December 1960, Bob Dylan dropped out of college.[1] On a snowy winter morning the next month, he left the Twin Cities with a few pieces of clothing in a suitcase, a guitar, a harmonica rack and a few bucks in his pocket, heading east "to find Woody Guthrie." Dylan played his first gig the very day he arrived in New York. By the end of the year, he had performed at one of the premier folk clubs in the United States.

This book focuses on the transformation of a Woody Guthrie wannabe into a folk and rock music icon. It emphasizes Dylan's first half dozen or so years in New York, when the city—and Greenwich Village in particular— had its most profound influence on him. It then follows his New York odyssey through the 1960s and into the first half of the 1970s, touching on his subsequent relationship with the city as he dropped by intermittently over the ensuing decades.

Robert Allen Zimmerman may have been born in the North Country cold-water port of Duluth and raised in landlocked Hibbing on the Mesabi Iron Range, living on a street called Seventh Avenue (a five-block stretch of the street is now called Bob Dylan Drive), but he was reborn as Bob Dylan in New York. As Dylan writes in *Chronicles*, the first volume of his memoirs, "New York City was the magnet—the force that draws objects to it."[2]

1

LOOKING FOR WOODY

Hey, hey, Woody Guthrie, I wrote you a song.
—Bob Dylan, "Song to Woody"

Bob Dylan arrived in New York City in late January 1961, during one of the coldest winters on record. The temperature was fourteen degrees Fahrenheit; nine inches of snow lay on the ground. A North Country boy, Dylan felt right at home.

Dylan had traveled from Minnesota in a four-door 1957 Impala sedan, dozing much of the way in the back seat. He came to New York, the biting wind hitting him smack in the face, to meet his hero, Woody Guthrie. He knew no one in the city, but he wasted no time getting a gig once he arrived. Like many a musician before and since, he made his way to Greenwich Village, America's historic bohemia. In fact, Dylan performed at the renowned Village coffeehouse Cafe Wha? the day he set foot in the city. "I was ready for New York," he commented years later.[3]

Dylan boasted that when he left Minnesota, he left the past behind. "I didn't think I had a past," he said. Of course, that was not quite true, but it made for good copy. Hungry for experience, he reinvented himself as the reincarnation of his spiritual father, Woody Guthrie, complete with guitar, harmonica and faux hayseed accent.[4]

Dylan soon mixed his newfound drawl with the hipster attitude of the Beats, infusing his language with an element of urban sophistication. Still, Guthrie remained his musical mentor. The first significant song he wrote, "Song to Woody," was composed "in five minutes" at the Mills Tavern on Bleecker Street on February 14, a few weeks after he arrived in New York.

Cheap and Safe

New York in the early 1960s was perched on the precipice of change, moving from one era—the supposed "innocence" of the Eisenhower years—to another—the dynamic but short-lived excitement of the Kennedy years. Indeed, the relatively short span between Eisenhower's election in 1952 and the arrival of the Beatles in America in 1964 ushered in a decade or so of social change that shook American society to its very core on many levels: politically, socially and economically. From peaceful civil rights demonstrations in the streets to racially tinged riots and the assassinations of Medgar Evers, Malcolm X, John F. Kennedy, Martin Luther King Jr. and Robert F. Kennedy, the 1960s started with a gentle whimper and ended with an explosive bang.

People made their way to New York from all over the country, and they still do, of course. But New York was different then in ways that are almost unimaginable today. For one thing, it was both cheap *and* safe. OK. New York prides itself nowadays as being the safest big city in the United States. Crime rates have plummeted over the last decade (they have risen, as in many American cities, during the 2020–21 COVID pandemic). But the cost of living, especially in Manhattan, is very steep. So steep, in fact, that if Dylan were arriving in New York today, he wouldn't be able to afford to live in Manhattan.

Not only were the rents cheap. Everything was cheap. It cost a nickel to ride the Staten Island Ferry. Even when Patti Smith came to town a few years later, in 1967, as a twenty-year-old exile from New Jersey, she could order a cup of coffee, a slice of toast and jam and one egg for as little as fifty cents. The city was safe enough for her to sleep on a bench in Central Park without fear of being harassed.[5]

Cultural attitudes in the early 1960s were different, too, and in rather unexpected ways, such as the city's unspoken dress code. With the exception of folks in Greenwich Village, most Manhattanites conformed to a strict and conventional wardrobe. Women and girls were expected to dress properly—no slacks and certainly no blue jeans—whether heading to the office or going about their business on an ordinary day. Businessmen always wore suits and ties to work. People in the outer boroughs dressed up when they went to Manhattan.

But down in the Village, befitting its anything-goes reputation, the rules governing not only dress and comportment but also behavior and social mores were much more easygoing. Villagers flouted respectable society, which basically meant they turned their collective backs on anything located above Fourteenth Street.

It was in the Village where Bobby Zimmerman would become the Bob Dylan we know.

FINDING WOODY IN DINKYTOWN

Dylan first discovered Woody Guthrie in Dinkytown, the small bohemian enclave adjacent to the University of Minnesota campus. Dylan had left his hometown of Hibbing in the spring of 1959; by that summer, he was in Minneapolis, some two hundred miles to the south, the first big city he spent any significant time in.

In September 1959, he enrolled at the University of Minnesota in Minneapolis, but he was an inattentive student at best. To even call Dylan a student is a stretch: he barely attended classes. "I just didn't feel like it," he later admitted. "I really didn't have time for study." Instead, he usually could be found at one of the neighborhood's local cafés. He was a regular performer at the Ten O'Clock Scholar, the popular Dinkytown coffeehouse located a few blocks from the university. He sang mostly traditional songs as well as Guthrie covers, including "This Land Is Your Land" and "Pastures of Plenty." In fact, he dropped out after only four quarters. (Even so, his name appears on the university's Wall of Discovery, along with the names of other creative alumni and faculty. Ironically, the word *student*, which appears by Dylan's name, is misspelled.)[6]

Ten O'Clock Scholar. Dylan was a regular at the popular Dinkytown coffeehouse. *Author collection.*

"The Times They Are A-Changin'." In 2015, the Brazilian street artist Eduardo Kobra completed a mural at the corner of Fifth and Hennepin in downtown Minneapolis that captured Dylan through three distinct phases of his life. The prolific Kobra has painted murals of other musicians, including David Bowie as Ziggy Stardust in Jersey City, New Jersey; Michael Jackson and "the 27 Club" (Janis Joplin, Kurt Cobain, Jim Morrison, Jimi Hendrix and Amy Winehouse—who all died at the age of twenty-seven) in New York; Tupac Shakur and the Notorious B.I.G. in Miami; and Muddy Waters in Chicago. *Photo by author.*

Dylan recalls that he was "stunned" the first time he heard Guthrie's voice. "All these songs together, one after another made my head spin. It made me want to gasp. It was like the land parted." From that day forward, Dylan obsessed about Guthrie the man and Guthrie the artist. He wanted to learn everything about him. Guthrie's memoir, *Bound for Glory*, which Dylan borrowed from a friend, "sang out" to him "like the radio." Whereas others might have thought Guthrie archaic and out of fashion, to Dylan, Guthrie's sound was more alive than anything he was hearing on the street or on the airwaves. Dylan made a personal vow: he decided he would sing only Guthrie songs and become the Oklahoman's disciple.[7]

Using Guthrie as a role model, Dylan developed a new persona, a hybrid invention that was part bohemian, part biker-poet, part ballad singer. Guthrie's image of the hard-traveling loner with a guitar and a way with words appealed to him. Dylan adjusted his accent to make it sound more Okie-like; he invented stories about being an orphan and riding the rails— just like his hero; he changed the way he dressed. He essentially became Woody Guthrie—for a time.

Dylan, the lackluster student, received his real education on the streets of Dinkytown. And even though he said that he identified more with *Bound for Glory* than *On the Road*, he nevertheless imbibed a steady diet of Beat literature, too: Gregory Corso and Lawrence Ferlinghetti in addition to Jack Kerouac and Allen Ginsberg.

In 2015, the Brazilian artist Eduardo Kobra finished his 160-foot wide, five-story mural of Dylan at the corner of Fifth and Hennepin in downtown Minneapolis as seen through three phases of his life: young Dylan, Dylan at the height of his fame and the older Dylan of the thin mustache and wide-brimmed hat.

It made sense that Greenwich Village appealed to Dylan. Dinkytown was a smaller version of Greenwich Village; it was the Minnesota equivalent of the Village. And it bears repeating that it was in Dinkytown where Robert Zimmerman honed his musical skills and started his transformation into Bob Dylan.

MAKING THE ROUNDS

When Dylan arrived in New York, he took the subway to Greenwich Village and went straight to the **Cafe Wha?** (**1**) at 115 MacDougal Street and Minetta Lane, a former horse stable and popular club with coffeehouse

Cafe Wha? Dylan made his Greenwich Village debut here shortly after he arrived in town. *Photo by author.*

roots. (It still offers live music of all types seven days a week.) He asked the owner, Manny Roth, if he could play. Singer Fred Neil booked the daytime shows at the time. (In 1965, Neil released his debut album, *Bleecker & MacDougal*, which featured a young Villager named John Sebastian on harmonica. Neil today is best known as the writer of "Everybody's Talkin'" from the soundtrack of the 1969 film *Midnight Cowboy*.) "He couldn't have been nicer," Dylan recalls. Dylan played something, and before you could say Mesabi Iron Range, he was told he could accompany Neil on harmonica during his sets. It was a modest beginning.[8]

It was at the Cafe Wha? and other Village coffeehouses that Dylan would blow "his lungs out for a dollar a day," as he wrote in one of his early songs, "Talkin' New York." The Cafe Wha? was described as a subterranean cavern, dimly lit and alcohol-free. It opened at noon and closed at four in the morning. The daytime acts were chaotic and amateurish, but Dylan didn't mind. He was glad to get out of the cold—North Country boy or no North Country boy—but he was even more appreciative to have a regular gig.

The audience at the Cafe Wha? consisted of an assortment of people: college students, suburbanites, secretaries on their lunch hour, sailors, tourists. The talent wasn't just musicians; they were comics, ventriloquists, poets, female impersonators, magicians—an odd but lively menagerie. By eight in the evening, though, the small stage was turned over to "the professionals," which, at that time, consisted of comedians such as Richard Pryor, Woody Allen, Joan Rivers and Lenny Bruce.

Dave Van Ronk Street in Sheridan Square. Singer, songwriter and guitarist Dave Van Ronk (1936–2002) was a Village mainstay. It wasn't for nothing that he was called the "Mayor of MacDougal Street," which also happens to be the title of his posthumous 2005 memoir, coauthored with Elijah Wald. *Photo by author.*

To Dave Van Ronk, the Minnesota native was "the scruffiest-looking fugitive from a cornfield I do believe I had ever seen." But he also thought the young Dylan was one of the funniest people he had ever seen—onstage at least. He compared Dylan's stage persona to no less than Charlie Chaplin—all nervous energy and studied mannerisms. Van Ronk and Dylan soon became fast friends: Van Ronk showed Dylan the ropes, took him to the Village clubs and even let Dylan crash on his couch (he was couch-surfing before the term was invented).[9] After Dylan moved into his own place in the Village, he spent time listening to records and playing cards with Van Ronk and his wife, Terri Thal, at their apartment at 180 Waverly Place. In 2004, a section of Sheridan Square in the Village was named Dave Van Ronk Street.

The gig at Cafe Wha? led to other gigs in other clubs. During those early weeks in the Village—and Dylan rarely left the Village in those days—Dylan played everywhere that he could: the Folklore Center, the Commons (later renamed the Fat Black Pussycat), the Lion's Head, the Caricature, Mills House, the Limelight, the Village Gate, Café Figaro, Caravan Café and the Third Side. He also played at folk song society meetings and for private gatherings, and he also tried out new material in Washington Square Park.

THE FOLK SCENE

Dylan arrived in New York at a crucial moment. Folk music was flourishing; for a musician whose hero was Woody Guthrie, New York was the only place to be.

According to Dave Van Ronk, the **Café Bizarre (2)** at 106 West Third Street was the first coffeehouse in the Village to feature folk music (a New York University Law School dormitory gobbled up the block in the 1980s). Rick Allmen, a Soho landlord, couldn't help but notice all the folk singers hanging out in the Village, and he thought it might be a wise economic decision to open a coffeehouse to provide a place for them to gather. The café opened in August 1957 with Odetta as the headliner. Two years later, Allmen was hawking copies of an independently produced album called *Assorted Madness* that featured Beat poetry and music by some of its performers. During its post-Beat days, the café even presented John Cale and Lou Reed of the Velvet Underground.

Café Bizarre ("Where the beat meet the elite," as an ad once stated; another read, "Be prepared for the unexpected") was located in a garage on Third Street that reportedly had once been Aaron Burr's stable. (Burr is best known today not as Thomas Jefferson's vice president but as the man who killed Alexander Hamilton in an 1804 duel, which was, of course, famously depicted in the hit Broadway musical *Hamilton*.) Either way, Van Ronk describes the ambiance as "cut-rate Charles Addams haunted house: dark and candlelit, with fake cobwebs." The waitresses looked like Morticia—the fictional matriarch of the Addams family—and wore fishnet stockings, with long straight hair and raccoon eyes. Bonnie Bremser, the wife of Village poet Ray Bremser and a waitress at the café, called it a "firetrap" that was "designed to hustle tourists." Dylan's description was more prosaic. He merely called it "an unusual beer and wine place on Third Street."[10] It also served food, such as the Bohemian Burger (melted cheddar cheese and bacon) for $1.10. The back of the café's menu featured a map of Village sites. It also boasted that the venue was available for "special occasion—also for weddings, divorces, wakes, bar mitzvas, brisses and sweet sixteens."

Another popular gathering place was **Mills House (3)** at 158 Bleecker Street (also listed as 160 Bleecker Street), also known as the Mills Tavern, a former hotel built in 1896 that consisted of 1,500 small rooms catering to men down on their luck. It is now an upscale apartment building called the Atrium, although the words *Mills House* can still be seen over the front door. In the late 1950s, though, the Mills was essentially a flophouse. Because of the sorry

Village Gate sign. In 1958, impresario Art D'Lugoff (1924–2009) opened the Village Gate, an iconic jazz club at the corner of Thompson and Bleecker Streets in Greenwich Village. The musical revue *Jacques Brel Is Alive and Well and Living in Paris* made its off-Broadway debut here. The Village Gate closed in 1994 and is now the location of Le Poisson Rouge, a music venue and multimedia cabaret. *Photo by author.*

condition of the building, music promoter Art D'Lugoff was able to negotiate a forty-eight-year lease at a reasonable cost for space in the former laundry room of the basement. D'Lugoff called it the Village Gate, and it soon became one of the premier live-music clubs in the Village. During its heyday—he opened it in 1958—the Village Gate hosted Odetta, Pete Seeger, Nina Simone, Aretha Franklin, Charles Mingus, Thelonious Monk and John Coltrane, among many others. D'Lugoff also booked off-Broadway productions in the space: *Jacques Brel Is Alive and Well and Living in Paris* debuted there.

During the height of the folk revival, the folk magazine *Broadside* sponsored a hootenanny on the first Sunday of every month at the Gate. Despite D'Lugoff's affiliation with the folk movement, Dylan never played there. In fact, when Dylan auditioned for a gig, D'Lugoff turned him down flat, believing he was simply a Woody Guthrie clone. It was only when Dylan began writing his own material that D'Lugoff became interested. By that time, Dylan had moved on.

After declaring bankruptcy, D'Lugoff closed the club in 1993 (the Village Gate sign is still there). In 2008, the venue reopened as Le Poisson Rouge, an eclectic and sophisticated cabaret; D'Lugoff served as its musical consultant until his death in 2009.

THE TROUBADOUR OF GREYSTONE

Dylan had come to New York specifically to meet Guthrie. "I thought it would be a nice gesture to visit him," he said. But by the time Dylan arrived, his hero was withering away from the ravages of Huntington's chorea at Greystone Hospital in Morristown, New Jersey. Getting to Greystone took much effort. Dylan caught the bus from the Port Authority Terminal in Midtown Manhattan and slowly made his way to the hospital, which he describes as a gloomy medieval fortress. He brought along a pack of Raleigh cigarettes as a gift and played Guthrie variations of his own songs, from "Do Re Mi" and "Dust Bowl Blues" to "Pretty Boy Floyd" and "Tom Joad."[11]

During his early days in New York, Dylan visited the Oklahoman often. On Saturday afternoons, Bob and Sidsel Gleason of East Orange, New Jersey, would bring Woody from Greystone to the Gleasons' nearby walk-up apartment so that he could visit with family and friends. Dylan listened in awe as Guthrie told stories—although in ill health, Guthrie could still muster up enough strength to entertain a crowd when the occasion called for it. Guests such as folklorist Alan Lomax, Guthrie's manager Harold Leventhal and various singers from the Greenwich Village folk scene would discuss the history of folk and sing countless versions of the classics. Dylan soon became Guthrie's favorite protégé. Whenever Woody requested a song, Dylan knew it. "The boy's got it!" Guthrie reportedly said, in sheer delight. "He sure as hell's got it!"[12]

During one visit, Guthrie told Dylan about boxes of lyrics and poems that Guthrie had written but had not yet been able to set to music. They were stored in Guthrie's house on Mermaid Avenue in Coney Island. Guthrie told Dylan he was welcome to them. Soon after, Dylan took the subway and got off at the last stop in Brooklyn. He looked for Guthrie's house but had difficulty finding it until he noticed a series of row houses across a field. Walking across the field, he realized that the soft ground under his feet had turned into a deep, marshy swamp. He sank into the muck down to his knees. Frozen to the bone and drenched, he eventually found the house and knocked on the door. The babysitter who answered told Dylan that Guthrie's wife, Marjorie, was not home but that his son Arlo, who would years later become a famous musician in his own right, was there. Arlo was just a young boy at the time and didn't know where the manuscripts were.

Arlo recalls Dylan as being a "sort of ragamuffin-type human with weird shoes and crazy sort of hair." Arlo was a bit put off by Dylan's appearance, even somewhat scared, but eventually, he said: "I took to him. I thought he had sort of neat shoes. They were like hiking boots. I figured he can't be a crook—not wearing hiking boots. So I invited him in. He showed me something on the harmonica. Didn't last probably more than ten or fifteen minutes. The girl [the babysitter] finally got the nerve to ask him to leave and come back sometime when my mother would be there." Much to his regret, Dylan never did record those lost Guthrie songs. Several decades later, the Chicago-based alt rock band Wilco and the English singer-songwriter-activist Billy Bragg did.[13]

ON AND OFF THE PARK

Folk was rooted in the musical traditions of the past, but in the late 1950s and early 1960s, it used the inspiration of the past to mount a challenge to the political and cultural status quo of the present. Within much of mainstream America, folk was denigrated as the music of outcasts and misfits; in the Village, however, words like *outcasts* and *misfits* were not insults.[14]

Folk singing in the Village got its start in **Washington Square Park (4)** in the mid-1940s, when a professional printer by the name of George Margolin started strumming a guitar and singing folk and left-leaning songs near the park's fountain. In fact, most musicians sang and played for free in the park or passed the basket around for spare change in the neighborhood coffeehouses. According to music critic David Hajdu, "the principal measure of success for the majority of folk singers was peer approval": they had to be "untainted by professionalism." Above all else, authenticity was lauded. But, as Tony Fletcher notes, it wasn't just folk singers who gathered in the park. There were also fire-eaters and fiddlers. The drunken poet and Village fixture Maxwell Bodenheim sold his poems by the sheet, and "Italian bands" performed "traditional songs for spare change" (the Village at that time, especially the South Village, was still a predominantly Italian neighborhood). The Village was truly a village. "Everybody knew everybody," says music critic Anthony DeCurtis, who grew up in the Village.

As the folk revival gathered steam, hundreds of young people congregated in the park on weekends to play their acoustic instruments and listen to each other play. In 1958, "Tom Dooley" by the Kingston Trio reached the top of the charts. With that success, folk music was transformed from a cult interest to a bona fide commercial success. Wave upon wave of tourists started to descend on the Village. The music became so popular that on weekend nights the police set up barricades on the streets to maintain control, especially along MacDougal Street. Every landlord eager to make a fast buck converted space—no matter how small—into a coffeehouse. All anyone needed to do was hang a sign announcing "Folk Music," and the cash registers started jingling. At the height of the "folk scare," as veteran musicians disparagingly called it, as many as forty coffeehouses operated in the Village, most of them within several blocks of MacDougal Street.

Sundays in Washington Square Park were special treats. People gathered to hear free concerts featuring all kinds of music. There were bluegrass players such as David Grisman and Eric Weissberg. Other musicians such as Maria Muldaur, Stefan Grossman and John Sebastian played folk, ragtime, blues, swing and jazz. Sebastian, at the time a thirteen-year-old living on nearby Washington Square West, recalls playing with Dylan and other musicians "whose names I didn't know, but who I saw every week." Dylan, still new in town, spent some Sunday afternoons in the park, describing it as a host to "a world of music" where poets "would rant and rave from the statues." He even attempted to write a song about the scene, "Down at Washington Square." Although Dylan never recorded or, for that matter, completely finished it, biographer Clinton Heylin theorizes that the song was a response to a police crackdown on folk singers in the park in April 1961, just three months after Dylan arrived in the city.

Banjo- and sandal-maker Allan Block ran one of the first centers for folk music in the Village: the **Allan Block Sandal Shop (5)** at 171 West Fourth Street, which opened in 1950. Part work space, part hangout, by the mid-1950s, the Sandal Shop was not only a meeting place for Villagers and tourists interested in folk culture but also the site of Saturday afternoon jam sessions where musicians on tour, including seminal figures in the folk and blues scenes such as Doc Watson, Clarence Ashley and Mississippi John Hurt, could unwind, trade songs and swap stories. Dylan occasionally stopped by.

ALONG MACDOUGAL

Cafe Wha? was simply a way station for Dylan. He had his sights on better, if not necessarily bigger, venues. These included the **Gaslight Café (6)**, 116 MacDougal Street, considered a premier venue for folk singers and Dylan's first important engagement in the city. Dylan historian Sean Wilentz goes so far as to call the Gaslight the Village equivalent of Carnegie Hall.

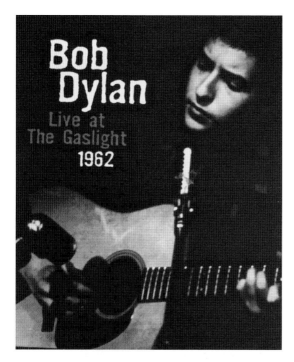

Left: *Live at the Gaslight 1962*. According to Dylan biographer Sean Wilentz, the ten tracks on the *Live at the Gaslight* CD were recorded during two separate sets between the singer's eponymous 1961 debut album and his 1963 *The Freewheelin' Bob Dylan*. On the liner notes, the producers apologize for the less than flawless production values, referring to the sound of street noise, the honking of cars and audience members singing along, or, gasp, even coughing. But all of that "noise" just adds to its charm. *Author collection*.

Below: Former site of the Gaslight. The Gaslight has been reincarnated in many forms. Here, it was the Alibi Bar & Lounge. *Photo by Theresa Albini*.

Located in a former coal cellar, the Gaslight was down a flight of stairs and next door to a bar at 114 MacDougal Street called the **Kettle of Fish (7)**. (The Kettle of Fish later moved to 130 West Third Street and is now at 59 Christopher Street; the Gaslight is now the Up & Up, a craft cocktail lounge.) Because of its proximity to the Gaslight, Kettle of Fish was a popular meeting place where folk singers between sets could relax, gossip and swap ideas and songs.

The Gaslight was owned by a "wild-looking" Brooklynite named John Mitchell. (For a short time, he also owned a Parisian-like coffeehouse called Le Figaro at 184–86 Bleecker Street before he sold it at a huge profit.) Mitchell was an entrepreneur of the first order. Because the ceiling was low, he lowered the floor. Rather than selling alcohol, as most Village bars did, he served sugary drinks and strong coffee—partly to ward off attention from the Mob. The Village was still an Italian neighborhood at the time, and many taverns relied on the Mafia to secure a liquor license and to protect them from monetary shakedowns from corrupt cops, who were no rarity in the neighborhood. Mitchell was a fierce critic of the men in blue as well as the gangsters who hovered around the edges of the scene.

A cabaret license was required for any venue that offered live entertainment. The coffeehouse owners thought that because they did not serve alcohol, they could steer clear of police troubles, but the cops raided the coffeehouses anyway. Perhaps because of Mitchell's stubborn refusal to play the game according to the rules, the police constantly raided the Gaslight. Still, he held his ground.

Because the Gaslight and other coffeehouses did not have liquor licenses, musicians would often sneak in booze in brown paper bags. Apparently, the coffee wasn't of the best quality. "Those coffeehouses," recalls Dave Van Ronk, "had the worst coffee I have ever encountered." The venues didn't make much money from selling coffee, but at least the rents were low.[15]

Despite its reputation as a good place to hear music, the Gaslight was dingy. When it first opened in the 1950s, it was known as a poets' café, a Beat hangout. Although writers from Allen Ginsberg and Gregory Corso to Lawrence Ferlinghetti read there at various times, Dylan's friend Bonnie Bremser remembers it as a place "for bad poetry." It became so synonymous with the Beats that television journalist Mike Wallace, of *60 Minutes* fame, brought a camera crew down to the café to conduct interviews with genuine "beatniks." (The footage appears in the 1963 low-budget film *The Greenwich Village Story*.)[16] The beatnik image was so prominent that the *Village Voice* ran a weekly ad for a "Rent-a-Beatnik" service: for a small price, it would

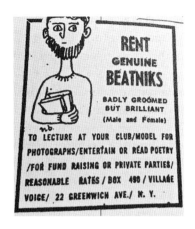

RENT
GENUINE
BEATNIKS
BADLY GROÓMED
BUT BRILLIANT
(Male and Female)
ꝴ.
TO LECTURE AT YOUR CLUB/MODEL FOR
PHOTOGRAPHS/ENTERTAIN OR READ POETRY
/FOR FUND RAISING OR PRIVATE PARTIES/
REASONABLE RATES / BOX 490 / VILLAGE
VOICE/ 22 GREENWICH AVE./ N. Y.

Rent-a-Beatnik. During the heyday of the Village coffeehouse scene, the beatnik image was so popular that the *Village Voice* ran a weekly "Rent-a-Beatnik" ad. *Author collection.*

send a bearded bohemian, complete with beret, to liven up middle-class parties.

Dimly lit, the Gaslight had bare brick walls, fake Tiffany lamps and exposed and leaky pipes that dripped onto the stage. At most, it could fit around 125 people. While Dylan was there, the pay was roughly sixty dollars per week—in cash. Noel Stookey, who later changed his first name to Paul and became one-third of Peter, Paul and Mary, was the emcee. A comedian, singer and guitar player who worked in a camera store during the day, Stookey did wild imitations and all kinds of sound effects, from a flushing toilet to clogged water pipes. Dylan thought he was very funny, if a bit aloof.

Dylan tried out new songs such as "A Hard Rain's A-Gonna Fall" in front of Gaslight audiences and performed folk and traditional standards. Between sets, he drank Wild Turkey and bottles of cold Schlitz next door at the Kettle of Fish or played cards in the Gaslight's upstairs room. To get to that room, patrons had to go through the kitchen, past a courtyard and up a fire escape.

Dylan recalls that the Kettle of Fish was usually packed with literary types, musicians and all kinds of characters, including "eclectic girls, non-homemaker types," as well as a "pistol-packing rabbi" and a "snaggle-toothed girl with a big crucifix between her breasts." Dylan would sit on a barstool and look out the window to the streets outside, watching the Villagers walk by, some famous—David Amram, Gregory Corso, Ted Joans, Fred Hellerman—most not. He would listen to the jukebox, too, which contained mostly jazz records. Dylan, always the contrarian, would drop a coin into the slot to hear Judy Garland singing Harold Arlen's "The Man that Got Away." Garland, the former Frances Gumm, hailed from Grand Rapids, Minnesota, about twenty miles from Dylan's hometown of Hibbing. "Listening to Judy was like listening to the girl next door," he reminisced. He felt an "emotional kinship" not only with Judy's voice but also with Arlen's songs—in Arlen's lonely lyrics, Dylan heard the sound of folk and the rural blues.[17]

Mitchell also owned the Commons, a café at 105 MacDougal Street. Opening in 1958 as a poetry café, it became a venue for an eclectic and wonderfully weird collection of performers, from Tiny Tim (he was a singing waiter) to Richie Havens. Mitchell later remodeled the café and, in 1962, renamed it the **Fat Black Pussycat (8)**. Since 1972, it has been a Mexican restaurant, Panchito's, but the faded Fat Black Pussycat sign is still visible on a brick wall above the restaurant at 13 Minetta Street. It was here that Dylan wrote the anthemic "Blowin' in the Wind" in, or so he claims, twenty minutes (originally, he said he had written it in ten).

In 2005, Columbia released *Bob Dylan Live at the Gaslight 1962*. Culled from two performances at the Gaslight in October 1962, the recording consists of sparkling performances of traditional folk songs ("Barbara Allen," "The Cuckoo [Is a Pretty Bird]"), as well as original material ("Don't Think Twice, It's All Right," "John Brown") and captures Dylan at the cusp of fame.

SUZE

In the summer of 1961, Dylan met Susan "Suze" Rotolo, a seventeen-year-old, dark-haired beauty. Her older sister, Carla, was Alan Lomax's personal assistant; Dylan used to visit Lomax's apartment on West Third Street, rummaging through his record collection—ethnomusicologist and filmmaker Harry Smith's *Anthology of American Folk Music* was a favorite. Years later, Smith would listen to Dylan's *Highway 61 Revisited* and *Blonde on Blonde* in his room at the Chelsea Hotel. Although she had seen him play around town, Rotolo didn't pay much attention to Dylan until July 29, 1961, when he performed at a marathon folk concert—twelve continuous hours of music—held at the **Riverside Church (9)**, 490 Riverside Drive, a handsome building on the Upper West Side near the Columbia University campus. Modeled after Chartres Cathedral, it was—and still is—known for its support of progressive causes.

In addition to Dylan, Pete Seeger and Dave Van Ronk performed, as did the Greenbriar Boys, Tom Paxton and Ramblin' Jack Elliott. The press reported that Dylan, who was still unknown at the time, hailed from Gallup, New Mexico, and "played the guitar and harmonica simultaneously, and with rural gusto." Dylan and Rotolo flirted backstage. They got a lift back to the Village with journalist Pete Karman, Dylan in the back seat with Suze and Carla. It was the beginning of a passionate, erratic and sometimes painful relationship.[18]

Rotolo was impressed by Dylan's intensity and endearing oddness. "He was funny, engaging…and…persistent," she recalls in her memoir, *A*

Riverside Church. Dylan performed at a marathon folk concert at the Upper West Side church near Columbia University's Morningside Heights campus. An interdominational church, Riverside opened in 1930 and was designed in the neo-Gothic style. Long associated with social justice issues, Riverside was designated a city landmark by the New York City Landmarks Preservation Commission in 2000. *Photo by author.*

Freewheelin' Time. Many of Dylan's songs (some loving, some bitter) were written for or inspired by her: "Boots of Spanish Leather," "Tomorrow Is a Long Time," "Restless Farewell," "Ballad in Plain D," "All I Really Want to Do" and "Don't Think Twice, It's All Right." When Rotolo died in 2011, the obituaries credited her as being Dylan's first muse.[19]

Dylan's relationship with Rotolo was his first serious love affair. Unfortunately, Rotolo's mother, Mary, didn't like Dylan all that much. She sublet a penthouse apartment at **One Sheridan Square (10)** in an eight-story building where Dylan stayed occasionally with a friend in a one-bedroom apartment. An off-Broadway theater called One Sheridan Square was located in the basement. There, Carla handled the lighting for the theater while Suze operated the concession stand, built sets and made props. Today, the Axis Theatre Company is located on the ground-floor level, but the space is perhaps best known as the site of the groundbreaking Café Society, Barney Josephson's supper club that, when it opened in 1938, became the first racially integrated nightclub in the United States. Billie Holiday was the opening-night act.

One night, during the run of Brendan Behan's play *The Hostage*, Rotolo was standing in the back of the theater watching the performance when Behan walked in drunk. He wandered onto the stage, waving his hands furiously and spoke to the actors in an incoherent haze. Then he was off—to the nearby **White Horse Tavern (11)**, 567 Hudson Street. Dylan was at the theater that night, too, and he followed the Irishman. He hoped to chat with him, but Behan was in no shape for a conversation.

Dylan and Rotolo became regulars at the White Horse. They especially enjoyed hearing the Clancy Brothers and Tommy Makem perform Irish rebel songs. "Those really moved me," Dylan said later. He became friends with the musicians and began to think more and more about writing his own songs. But what to write about? During an interview in 2007, Liam Clancy said that despite their obvious differences—a Catholic from rural Ireland, a Jew from a small midwestern town—he and Dylan shared similar motives. "People who were trying to escape repressed backgrounds, like mine and Bob Dylan's, were congregating in Greenwich Village. It was a place [where] you could be yourself, where you could get away from the directives of the people who went before you, people who you loved but who you knew had blinkers on."[20]

The White Horse opened in 1880 as a longshoreman's bar, a far cry from the bohemian and literary associations that later brought it fame. It is closely linked to the Welsh poet Dylan Thomas, who famously drank himself to death there, or so it was once thought. (It is now believed that his untimely death, although aggravated by alcohol, was complicated by other health-related factors.)

In addition to Thomas, Dylan and the Clancy Brothers, other well-known patrons included Jack Kerouac (who was thrown out of the bar for his rowdy behavior), Mary Travers, Norman Mailer, James Baldwin, Delmore Schwartz, Richard Fariña, the activist Jane Jacobs (this stretch of Hudson Street, in fact, is also known as Jane Jacobs Way) and the late gonzo journalist Hunter S. Thompson. But it is the association with Dylan Thomas that is the strongest. He is commemorated in numerous ways at the Horse. In the middle room, a portrait based on an iconic photograph of him taken by Bunny Adler hangs next to an old clock. In the portrait, Thomas stands at the counter surrounded by other patrons, a cigarette in his left hand, and looks straight at you as if he is about to buy you a drink. An undated poster for a production of his play *Under Milkwood* hangs on a wall.

But on at least one significant level, things have changed since Dylan Thomas drank here: "Intoxicated Persons Will Not Be Served," a sign warns.

Dylan Thomas. The Welsh poet Dylan Thomas is commemorated in the middle room of the White Horse Tavern. Bob Dylan was a regular at the former longshoreman's bar and was especially fond of listening to the Clancy Brothers and Tommy Makem perform Irish rebel songs. *Photo by author.*

IZZY'S CATHEDRAL

Dylan spent many days and nights at the **Folklore Center** **(12)** at 110 MacDougal Street. "The citadel of Americana folk music," as he called it, was located up a flight of stairs over what is now a nail salon.[21]

In April 1957, Israel "Izzy" Young opened the Folklore Center. Young was a twenty-nine-year-old who wore horn-rimmed glasses and spoke with a thick Brooklyn accent. In addition to running the store, he also produced folk concerts at the Town Hall in Midtown Manhattan and on university campuses. Although it was always a busy place, the Folklore Center was, as David Hajdu points out, "barely profitable." Folk singer and radio host Oscar Brand once called Young "the worst businessman in the world." Still, the Folklore Center was the social hub of the Village folk scene: musicians were constantly stopping by to hear the latest folk news and gossip. Dylan listened to records in the back room, with its potbellied wood-burning stove. He savored the laid-back atmosphere, his ear attuned to the conversations swirling around him.[22] Young seemed to know everyone on the folk scene and coffeehouse circuit. In *Rainbow Quest*, Ronald Cohen called him "the Samuel Pepys of the Revival."

Dylan compared the Folklore Center to "an ancient chapel, like a shoe-box sized institute." It carried an esoteric collection of songs: sea shanties, Civil War songs, cowboy songs, union songs and books and various types of pamphlets. It also sold instruments: dulcimers, banjos, kazoos, penny whistles, acoustic guitars and mandolins. Records and instruments hung in its wide plate-glass windows. Concerts were held in the front of the store at least once a month. Some of the best and most famous folk singers played here, including Clarence Ashley, Mance Lipscomb, Tom Paley and Erik Darling. The Folklore Center was, for all intents and purposes, a folk clearinghouse. Dylan was so taken with it that

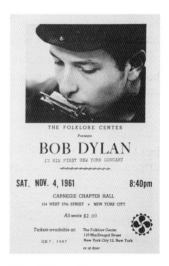

"The Folklore Center presents Bob Dylan in his first New York concert. November 4, 1961, at Carnegie Chapter Hall." Izzy Young (1928–2019), who owned the Folklore Center in the Village, was a prominent figure in New York City folk circles until he moved to Sweden. From 1973 until his death, he ran the Folklore Centrum, the Swedish equivalent of the center, in Stockholm. *Author collection.*

30

he paid homage to it in song—"Talking Folklore Center Blues." Young sold the printed song as a broadside.[23]

Izzy Young promoted Dylan's first professional concert at the two-hundred-seat **Carnegie Chapter Hall (13)**, 881 Seventh Avenue, on Saturday, November 4, 1961. Located in the same building as the prestigious Carnegie Hall, it is now known as Kaplan Space and is used primarily for rehearsals. (Dylan first appeared at Carnegie Hall itself in late September 1962 as part of a larger hootenanny bill.) The traditional Appalachian singer Jean Ritchie, who was in the audience that November night, recalls only "six girls in the place. That was the complete audience." Ritchie underestimates, but not by much, since only fifty-three people attended in the three-hundred-seat hall. (In the documentary *Bob Dylan: In & Out of the Folk Revival 1961–1965*, Young says the number was fifty-two, not fifty-three.) Dylan walked on stage late and, according to Ritchie, "talked about what a little country boy he was and how he got lost on the subway. Then he started tuning his instruments. We thought, 'Poor thing.'"[24]

The sparse turnout didn't seem to faze Dylan. A nearby table held twenty harmonicas. He began playing with each one, trying to find the one with the right sound. He sang a selection of traditional and blues standards, including "Pretty Peggy-O," "In the Pines," "Gospel Plow," "1913 Massacre," "Backwater Blues," "Long Time A-Growin'" and "Fixin' to Die." He was paid ten or twenty dollars for his effort. Some of these songs would soon appear on his debut album.

Although the concert could hardly be described as a success, it provided Dylan with some exposure above Fourteenth Street, the traditional northern boundary of Greenwich Village. A week later, another folk singer also appeared in a concert uptown, but to a vastly different response. Joan Baez performed in front of a sold-out audience at Town Hall. Her second album, *Joan Baez, Volume 2*, had just been released.

POSITIVELY FOURTH STREET

For months, Dylan slept on couches and on the floors of generous Villagers who offered him a place to rest. Dave Van Ronk and his wife, Terry Thal, were especially big-hearted. During his early days in New York, Dylan lodged with a middle-aged couple, Eve and Mac MacKenzie, on Twenty-Eighth Street. The MacKenzies were friends of Woody Guthrie and treated Dylan like a long-lost prodigal son.

Eventually, Dylan found his own space, a one-bedroom apartment on the third floor of a red-brick four-story railroad flat, built in 1910 and located at **161 West Fourth Street (14)** for $60 a month (in 2015, the apartment was sold for a considerably higher $6 million). He and Suze Rotolo moved into the flat in December 1961, shortly after Dylan recorded his eponymous debut album. "It wasn't much, just two rooms above Bruno's spaghetti parlor, next door to the local record store and a furniture supply shop on the other side," Dylan recalls in *Chronicles*. It had a "tiny" bedroom, "more like a large closet," Dylan says, "and a kitchenette, a living room with a fireplace and two windows that looked over fire escapes and small courtyards." According to Rotolo, the small bedroom was located behind the main room, the hardwood floors painted gray "to make the worn floors look better." There was plenty of sun in the summer, but it was cold in the winter. Their unit faced the back of the building and overlooked an "unkempt" garden behind a pizzeria next door.[25]

On the ground floor was the Door Store, which sold unfinished furniture. O'Henry's, a restaurant too expensive for the couple to frequent, was down the street. Allan Block's Sandal Shop was up the street. If a musician didn't have an instrument available to participate in the impromptu jam sessions held there, he or she could always go next door to the **Music Inn (15)**, 169 West Fourth Street, and ask to borrow one. Rotolo describes the Music Inn, established in 1958, as "an impossibly cluttered store that sold every kind of musical instrument ever made in the entire world…." It still does. A leftover from the old folk-era Village, it boasts noncommittal hours (Monday through Saturday "some time before 12 p.m." and "some time after 6:30 p.m."), and it stocks all kinds of instruments from around the world, floor to ceiling, at reasonable prices. Jeff, the long-haired, bearded and bespectacled owner, was there when Dylan was around. When I first dropped by, he told me he was sick of answering questions about Dylan, adding that he didn't particularly like Dylan. He thought Bob Dylan was a pest: Dylan used to come in to see if the store carried his records and never bought anything.

In her memoir of those years, Rotolo recalls that on Thompson near Bleecker was a shop that sold live chickens that were kept in cages and chicken coops piled on top of each other. When she and Dylan walked home in the wee hours of the morning, they would hear "the roosters crowing at the break of dawn," borrowing (perhaps) a lyric from Dylan's "Don't Think Twice, It's All Right." They would walk up Bleecker, crossing Sixth Avenue, to **Zito's Bakery (16)**, 259 Bleecker Street at Cornelia Street, which had a coal-fired brick oven in the basement. At night, the

A cornucopia of instruments and album covers are on display at the Music Inn on West Fourth Street, a short walk from Dylan's Greenwich Village apartment. *Photo by author.*

bakers would hand out fresh hot bread to hungry passersby.[26] (In the mid-1960s, Frank Sinatra reportedly banged on the door of the shop early one morning requesting a freshly baked loaf of bread.) The Sicilian-born Anthony Zito opened the bakery on December 1, 1924. Two weeks later,

Zito's Bakery. A popular Greenwich Village fixture until it closed in 2004. *Author collection.*

Zito's son Julio was born in the back room. Zito's was a neighborhood landmark until it closed in May 2004, due to a combination of rising rents and coal prices and changing diets.

Although only nineteen, Dylan was fast becoming known around the Village. But which Dylan were people greeting? His persona was always changing, always in flux. He told an endless variety of tall tales. At various

By the Way #1

The Woody Guthrie Foundation / the Woody Guthrie Center

For many years, the Woody Guthrie Archives were housed at the Woody Guthrie Foundation at 250 West Fifty-Seventh Street, down the street from Carnegie Hall. (In 2010, the foundation moved to 125–31 East Main Street, Mount Kisco, New York, about forty miles north of Manhattan.) On the shelves were bronze busts of Guthrie and his son Arlo; his friend and colleague Pete Seeger (who died in 2014); folk singers Judy Collins, Leadbelly, Ronnie Gilbert (who died in 2015) and Lee Hayes; and Guthrie's protégé, Bob Dylan—all created by Natalie Leventhal, the wife of Guthrie's manager, Harold Leventhal. The foundation was established in 1972 as a nonprofit organization that acts as the guardian of Guthrie's archives, the largest collection of material on Guthrie in the world. The collection contained more than fifteen thousand items, including original song lyrics (Guthrie left behind some 2,400 lyrics that had not been set to music), notebooks, diaries, manuscripts, correspondence, personal papers, artwork, films and recordings. In 1998 and 2000, the English folk-punk singer Billy Bragg and the American alternative folk band Wilco added music to about thirty of Guthrie's lyrics and released *Mermaid Avenue* and *Mermaid Avenue, Volume II* (named in honor of the Coney Island street where Guthrie once lived). In 2015, the founders dissolved the foundation. Two years earlier, in 2013, the Woody Guthrie Center opened in Tulsa, Oklahoma. It houses the Woody Guthrie Archives. It also contains the Phil Ochs Papers and the Ronald D. Cohen Folk Music Reference Book Collection. The building housing the archives operated as the Tulsa Paper Company from 1922 to 1980. Every year, the center announces the Woody Guthrie Prize. Recipients have included Bruce Springsteen (2021), Joan Baez (2020), Chuck D (2019), John Mellencamp (2018), Norman Lear (2017), Kris Kristofferson (2016), Mavis Staples (2015) and Pete Seeger (2014).

times, he said he was a miner or an orphan from New Mexico, or that he had been raised in numerous foster homes. Other times, he said he had Sioux Indian blood in him, which accounted for his exotic looks. His relatives were gamblers or thieves—perhaps both. He had lived in Oklahoma, Iowa, the Dakotas, Kansas and along the Mississippi River. At one point, he said he had joined a carnival at the age of thirteen and had seen a good part of the American Southwest. He had even played the piano on the early records of Elvis Presley. Todd Haynes's 2007 film *I'm Not There*, which depicts Dylan as seen through six different personas, captures the singer's magpie nature and the kind of identity games he has played over the decades. "You can go anywhere when you're someone else," he said years later.[27]

2

I IS SOMEONE ELSE

ylan first met Joan Baez on April 10, 1961, at the Monday "hoot
night" at **Gerde's Folk City (17)**, 11 West Fourth Street. Although
Baez was only six months older than Dylan, by the time she met him
she was already a star. Baez and her sister Mimi were in town to protest a
community measure meant to restrict folk singing in Washington Square
Park. A screaming headline in the *New York Mirror*, "3000 Beatniks Riot in
Village," was typical of mainstream attitudes toward so-called beatniks and
folkies. Joan and Mimi arrived too late for the Sunday rally but stayed on to
attend the Folk City gathering the following night.

All the major Village folk figures were there: Doc Watson, Gil Turner,
Dave Van Ronk. Dylan performed several Guthrie songs that night, which
impressed Baez. She sang several numbers, too. Dylan, though, seemed less
interested in listening to Joan than in flirting with her younger sister Mimi.
But he did ask the dark-haired Joan to go outside to the sidewalk in the
cold, damp night air so he could play a song for her. "Of course," she said.
He borrowed her Gibson guitar and sang the composition he had written
for Guthrie, "Song for Woody." It was an awkward start to an awkward
relationship.[28]

She was the queen of folk, he the wannabe prince. When Baez made the
cover of *Time* magazine in November 1962, Dylan was still referred to as
"a promising young hobo." Yet their friendship lingers to this day. When
a documentary on Baez was broadcast on public television in 2009, there
was Dylan commenting on her ("I was sorry to see our relationship end")

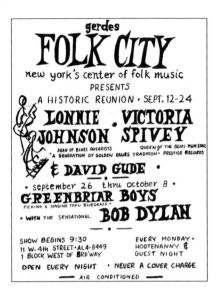

Flyer for Gerde's Folk City, 1961. The main attractions at this particular show were blues guitarist Lonnie Johnson (1889–1970) and blues singer Victoria Spivey (1906–1976), both of whom were influences on Dylan. According to Michael Gray, Dylan once said about Spivey, "Oh man, I loved her….I learned so much from her I could never put into words." A few days after the Johnson and Spivey reunion, "the sensational Bob Dylan" made his Folk City debut with the Greenbriar Boys on September 26, 1961. *Author collection.*

and, endearingly, calling her "Joanie." They shared the stage in 2010 when both appeared at a concert at the White House in honor of the civil rights movement, she singing "We Shall Overcome," he "The Times They Are A-Changin'."[29]

Gerde's Folk City, which officially opened on June 1, 1960, was the premier folk club in the United States (the building no longer exists) and booked nationally known folk singers. (Prior to opening Gerde's, Izzy Young and a businessman named Tom Prendergast operated the Fifth Peg there.) Housed in a six-story brownstone building erected in 1889, the space included a small elevated stage against a back wall; an oak-beam partition separated the bar area from the restaurant and the performance area. In front of the stage were tables and chairs. It was a tight fit. "If there were more than three people onstage at the same time," recalls Rotolo in her memoir, "it was a crowd."[30]

Struggling and unknown singers were encouraged to perform on Monday Hootenanny Nights. During one of those nights, Dylan met an "exotic, dark haired" woman named Camilla Adams who, he thought, looked like the actress Ava Gardner and lived on the top floor of a large apartment building on Fifth Avenue near Washington Square Park. Dylan thinks it was Adams who put a good word in for him with Gerde's owners, the Italian-immigrant siblings Mike and John Porco. Otherwise, Mike Porco may not have given Dylan the time of day; initially, he wasn't impressed with the Minnesotan. In any case, Dylan was hired in April 1961 for a two-week booking opposite the

BY THE WAY #2

Inside Llewyn Davis

The early days of the Village folk scene are beautifully depicted in Joel and Ethan Coen's evocative 2013 film *Inside Llewyn Davis*. Inspired by Dave Van Ronk's autobiography, *The Mayor of MacDougal Street*, it stars Oscar Isaac as the Van Ronk–like character, a struggling folk singer making the coffeehouse circuit before Dylan's arrival in Greenwich Village. Although modeled after Van Ronk, Isaac looks and sounds nothing like him. Whereas Isaac's singing voice is a warm and appealing tenor, Van Ronk was known for his gruff, bluesy sound.

It was an intentional choice on the part of the filmmakers, as it allowed them the leeway to explore what they wanted and in the way they wanted to explore it, using Van Ronk's memoir primarily as a skeleton to hang their story on and scouring the book mostly for local flavor and colorful anecdotes. The movie title itself is a play on Van Ronk's 1964 album, *Inside Dave Van Ronk*, which consists of traditional songs, from "House Carpenter"—an early Dylan favorite—to "Silver Dagger" and whose cover includes a cat (cats are prominently featured in the film). The artwork of Llewyn's solo album, *Inside Llewyn Davis*, by designer Gregory Hill briefly appears on screen. It mimics the Van Ronk album cover down to the same pose: Davis holds a cigarette in his right hand, his left hand thrust in his trouser pocket—but, ironically, without the cat. The design even uses Van Ronk's same lettering font.

On Van Ronk's album cover, the singer stands outside the swinging doors of McSorley's Old Ale House (15 East Seventh Street). McSorley is famous for many reasons (aside from being a great old Irish pub). Joseph Mitchell, the chronicler of the Village bohemian Joe Gould, frequented it and wrote an essay about it in 1940, "The Old House at Home." (He even had his own table—"Joe's table" was the second one from the window.) Woody

Guthrie was known to tipple a drink or two here, as did Dylan Thomas when he was in town. The Ashcan artist John Sloan painted a glorious portrait of it, *McSorley's Bar*, in 1912, and in 1925, e.e. cummings wrote a poem about it, "Snug and Warm Inside McSorley's."

Isaac's character does sing some songs associated with Van Ronk, including "Fare Thee Well (Dink's Song)," "Hang Me, Oh Hang Me" and "Green Rocky Road," and emulates his distinctive guitar style. He also shares Van Ronk's working-class roots and background, including his connection to the Merchant Marines. Also like Van Ronk, Davis loves and respects traditional music.

Numerous characters in the film are inspired or loosely based on other real-life figures: the singing duo Jim and Jean Berkey (Justin Timberlake and Carey Mulligan) on Peter, Paul and Mary, although Jim's bearded look more resembles the New England singer and folklorist Paul Clayton, who was a key influence on early Dylan. Gate of Horn owner Bud Grossman (F. Murray Abraham) is a model for Dylan's manager, Albert Grossman. (On the other hand, Barney Hoskyns suggests he represents the goateed Mitch Miller, then the A&R chief for Columbia Records.) In one of the more humorous set pieces in the movie, Davis makes his way to Chicago and auditions for Grossman. The song he chooses, though, is a rendition of the bleakly beautiful Child ballad "The Death of Queen Jane" (with its echoes of Dylan's own "Queen Jane Approximately"). After Davis finishes the song, the poker-faced Grossman offers a dry, "I don't see a lot of money here." (Something similar happened to Van Ronk, with the real Grossman muttering an equally dismissive, "I've got Muddy Waters and Memphis Slim here. What do I need with *you*?")

Other characters and their (roughly) real-life equivalents include Mel Novikoff (Jerry Grayson) as Moses "Moe" Asch, founder of Folkways Records; Pappi Corsicato (Max Casella) as Mike Porco, who ran Gerde's Folk City; Troy Nelson (Stark Sands) as singer-songwriter Tom Paxton; and the pseudo-cowboy-hat-wearing

Inside Llewyn Davis press kit. The Coen brothers' 2013 film starred Oscar Isaac as the Dave Van Ronk–like character. Other cast members included Carey Mulligan, John Goodman, Garrett Hedlund, Justin Timberlake and Adam Driver. The film's publicity department created a sixty-eight-page booklet that intentionally emulated the style of the influential *Sing Out!* magazine (published from May 1950 to 2014), down to the smallest details, including the price (seventy-five cents). It also contained five terrific essays on the Village folk scene by Robert Christgau, Elijah Wald, John Jeremiah Sullivan, Sean Wilentz and David Hajdu. *Author collection.*

Village folk singer Al Cody (Adam Driver) as Ramblin' Jack Elliott. A version of the Aran sweater–clad Clancy Brothers is here, too.

The filmmakers meticulously tried to re-create the New York City immortalized by the artwork on Dylan's *The Freewheelin' Bob Dylan.* "You can feel the slushy, cold New York winter in that photo," said cinematographer Bruno Delbonnel. Since the Gaslight is long gone, production designer Jess Gonchor had to find a proper alternative, converting an abandoned warehouse in the Crown Heights neighborhood of Brooklyn into the famed coffeehouse. "We lowered the height of the ceiling, constructed arches, brought in the period furniture and fixtures, and the result was that you really felt you were in a dingy Village club circa 1961." One of the songs that Davis sings in the film, "Dink's Song," is the same song that Dylan performed back in his Minnesota days. Ewan MacColl's "Shoals of Herring" and Dominic Behan's "The Auld Triangle" (but made famous by his playwright brother Brendan in the latter's 1954 play *The Quare Fellow*) are songs that Dylan would have known from his early days in the Village and songs that he and members of The Band taped in the basement of Big Pink, the house near Woodstock. Finally,

Llewyn's Welsh name echoes that of the Welsh poet Dylan Thomas (theories vary on whether or not Dylan took his name from the Welshman). In the film, "The Auld Triangle" is sung by Marcus Mumford, Justin Timberlake, Chris Thile and others. In January 1963, Dylan performed "Hang Me" and three other songs ("Blowin' in the Wind," "The Cuckoo" and "The Ballad of the Gliding Swan," the latter an update of a Scottish Border Ballad song) on *Madhouse on Castle Street*, a BBC television show. The trip was not only his first time in England but was also the first time he had traveled outside North America. The journey took place midway through his recording of the *Freewheelin'* sessions. He was exposed to several London coffeehouses and folk clubs, including the iconic Bunjie's Coffee House and Folk Cellar, housed in a four-hundred-year old wine cellar and located off Charing Cross Road, and the Troubadour in Earls Court. He met the influential English folk singer Martin Carthy. It was Carthy who introduced him to the traditional English ballads "Lord Franklin" and "Scarborough Fair." In typical Dylanesque fashion, he soon would transform them into "Bob Dylan's Dream" and "Girl from the North Country," respectively.

At the film's conclusion, as Davis leaves the Gaslight, he sees a young Bob Dylan (Ben Pike) onstage, harmonica holder hanging from his neck, who sings, "Oh it's fare thee well…'": Dylan before he set the world on fire.

bluesman John Lee Hooker. By then, Dylan was no longer performing in Woody's long shadow. Because Dylan was still underage, Porco signed Dylan's cabaret and union contracts, effectively acting as his guardian. Mike, says Dylan, was the "Sicilian father that I never had." In the audience on his debut night were Dave Van Ronk, radio host Oscar Brand and Tom Paxton. After his residency ended, Dylan had high expectations. He thought that the great men of the music industry would court him.[31]

In the audience when Dylan played at Gerde's five months later, in September 1961, was thirty-three-year-old Robert Shelton (real name, Robert Shapiro) of the *New York Times*. Shelton, a Villager—he lived on Waverly Place across the street from Van Ronk—would later write a major biography of Dylan, *No Direction Home*. Among the songs Dylan performed that night were "900 Miles," House of the Risin' Son," "Dink's Song" and a few of his own, including "Talkin' Bear Mountain Picnic Massacre Blues." In between sets, Shelton interviewed Dylan. His review of Dylan's performance, which ran on September 29, 1961, couldn't have come at a better time. Shelton described Dylan as resembling "a cross between a choir boy and a beatnik." Although his voice was "anything but pretty," Shelton felt there was no doubt that the young singer was "bursting at the seams with talent." He admitted that although Dylan would not appeal to "every taste, his music-making has the mark of originality and inspiration all the more noteworthy for his youth." The reporter quickly realized Dylan's talent for exaggeration—"I had the strange feeling he was putting me on," Shelton confessed—but it didn't seem to bother him. "It matters less where he has been," Shelton concluded, "than where he is going, and that would seem to be straight up."[32]

Dylan and Rotolo bought the early edition of the *Times* that contained Shelton's review at a **newspaper kiosk (18)** on Sheridan Square and went across the street to an all-night deli to read it before returning to the stand to buy even more copies. The kiosk is still there, but the old wooden structure is hidden behind a shiny modern veneer.

The Aristocrat

Dylan had dreams of recording for Folkways Records, then located at 165 West Forty-Sixth Street. "That was the label I wanted to be on. That was the label that put out all the great records."

Folkways Records was founded in 1947 by Moses "Moe" Asch, the son of Sholem Asch, the influential Yiddish novelist and dramatist. The record label's purpose was simple yet ambitious: to document the music that the larger commercial labels largely ignored. At one point, Folkways was the largest folk label in the United States. Through ups and downs, Asch remained at the helm—in addition to being president, he was also the label's talent scout, engineer and "sometimes shipping clerk"—until his death in 1986. The following year, Smithsonian bought the label.

Bob Dylan admired Asch, but despite the many Dylan boosters in the Village who arranged for Asch to meet him, Asch was not impressed enough with the young man to sign him.[33] According to David Hajdu, Asch didn't even recall meeting Dylan. Meanwhile, the smaller record companies in town were snatching up folk singer after folk singer. Prestige had Van Ronk,

Elektra had Judy Collins and Vanguard had Baez and Ramblin' Jack Elliott. "Nobody wanted to touch Dylan," Young told Hajdu. "All the geniuses— none of them thought he was good enough." Instead, it took another producer, John Hammond, to sign the young singer.

John Hammond, who lived in the Village in a MacDougal Street townhouse, became aware of Dylan at a party at the Texas folk singer Carolyn Hester's apartment. A legendary Columbia producer and talent scout, Hammond had discovered and/or recorded Bessie Smith, Billie Holiday, Cab Calloway, Count Basie, Benny Goodman and Lionel Hampton and would later add Aretha Franklin and Bruce Springsteen to his list.

Carolyn Hester was married to folk singer Richard Fariña. (Fariña divorced Hester and, in April 1963, married Joan's sister, Mimi Baez. He died in a motorcycle accident three years later at the age of twenty-nine.) Hester asked Dylan to play harmonica on a few songs that were scheduled to appear on her debut album for Columbia. Hammond first met Dylan at a rehearsal with Hester's backup band. The musicians included Bruce Langhorne on guitar, Bill Lee on bass and Dylan on harmonica, but Dylan also played some guitar and sang harmony vocals. Before leaving Hester's apartment, Hammond asked Dylan, in passing, if he recorded for anyone. Dylan shook his head. Despite the perfunctory nature of their meeting, Hammond came away impressed with the young man. "What a wonderful character, playing guitar and blowing mouth harp, he's gotta be an original," Hammond thought.[34]

After reading the *New York Times* review of the Gerde's show, Hammond told Dylan he would like to record him. Dylan agreed, as nonchalantly as possible, even as his heart was pounding beneath the cool façade. "Inside I was in a state of unstable equilibrium, but you wouldn't have known it." Hammond's account is slightly different. Hammond asked Dylan whether he could write and sing; when Dylan responded affirmatively to both, Hammond invited him up to the studio. After Dylan sang just one song, the humorous "Talkin' New York," Hammond offered him a contract.[35]

Dylan later described Hammond as belonging to a "pure American aristocracy." He was a Vanderbilt—the great-great-grandson of Cornelius Vanderbilt—and Hammond had grown up in the most rarefied of atmospheres. The quintessential blueblood, he attended the best schools and lived a life of ease. But he deliberately traveled in bohemian circles, and his love of jazz, spirituals and the blues colored every aspect of his life. When Hammond placed a contract in front of him, Dylan signed it without paying much attention to the details and without the benefit of a lawyer.[36]

"Columbia was one of the first and foremost labels in the country and for me to even get my foot in the door was serious," he said. At the time, it was rare for a major record label to even consider signing a folk singer. Hammond told Dylan that he saw him as belonging to a tradition. Hammond then looked at a calendar, selected a date for the recording session and asked Dylan to give some thought as to what he wanted to play.[37]

Dylan couldn't believe his good fortune. All the other folk labels had turned him down, and here was the great John Hammond asking him to come over to Columbia. But, as the literary critic Louis Menand points out, "Hammond didn't sign Dylan on a whim; he signed him…because he had a chance to sign Baez and lost her to Vanguard. His reputation for picking winners was in jeopardy; folk was hot, and he needed a folksinger."[38]

Enter the Bear

In 1956, in the early days of the fledgling folk scene, a Chicago businessman named Albert Grossman—nicknamed the "Bear" because of his girth and brusque manner—opened the Gate of Horn folk club on the city's Near North Side. Three years later, during one of his numerous visits to the East Coast music clubs, Grossman saw Joan Baez perform in a Cambridge coffeehouse—she played at such venues as Cafe Yana and Club 47—and was so impressed with her that he arranged for her to play a two-week gig at the Chicago club. There she met the folk singer and guitarist Bob Gibson, the club's house singer. The musicians hit it off. In fact, Baez has admitted that she had a crush on Gibson at the time.

In July 1959, Grossman, along with the Boston-based jazz impresario and club owner George Wein, established the Newport Folk Festival. (Wein died on September 13, 2021, at age ninety-five.) The two-day festival featured such notable folk singers as Pete Seeger, the Kingston Trio, the bluegrass virtuoso Earl Scruggs and the blues duo of Sonny Terry and Brownie McGhee, as well as Bob Gibson. A mostly young crowd of thirteen thousand people attended the opening-day performances. The next evening, a Sunday, Baez made her debut at the festival when Gibson invited the then-unknown singer to perform along with him, introducing her as "a young lady from Boston." The intensity and sincerity of her performance, along with her unadorned and unusual combination of Mexican and Scottish beauty, left the audience spellbound.

More than a year later, in November 1960, Baez made a triumphant solo appearance at the festival. Her star was on the rise; in fact, she was considered among the most promising talents on the folk scene. Grossman ran in some of the same folk circles as Baez. After he sold his interest in the Gate of Horn, he moved to New York and became a manager. He quickly, through aggressive tactics and numerous connections in the industry, put together an impressive list of clients, which eventually included Bob Gibson and Hamilton Camp; Odetta; Peter, Paul and Mary; and, in August 1962, Bob Dylan. Grossman continued to represent Dylan until 1970.

Although he never managed her directly—but not through lack of trying—Grossman persuaded Baez to meet with Hammond at Columbia. Hammond tried to sign Baez, but she had a strong distaste for the big record companies, preferring the artistic freedom promised at the smaller labels, and thus declined Hammond's offer, choosing the independent label Vanguard instead, which was located on West Fourteenth Street off Eighth Street (the "low-rent northwest corner of Greenwich Village," as David Hajdu described it in *Positively 4th Street*).

IN THE STUDIO

Hammond had high expectations for Dylan. After all, he had a reputation to maintain. He had a lot riding on Dylan—not the least that he wanted to prove to the executives at Columbia that he still had the golden touch.

Hammond gave Dylan several unreleased recordings from the Columbia vault that he thought might be of interest. One of them was *King of the Delta Blues* by Robert Johnson. It was the first time Dylan heard Johnson, and he could hardly contain his excitement. He had felt the same way when he heard Guthrie for the first time.

Dylan went into **Columbia's Studio A (19)** at 799 Seventh Avenue to record his debut album on November 20 and 22, 1961. He made his first five albums in that studio; even when it was renamed A&R Studios, he continued to use it. *Bob Dylan* was recorded in two three-hour sessions. Released in March 1962, it consists of thirteen mostly traditional songs along with two originals, "Talkin' New York" and "Song to Woody," both strongly influenced by Guthrie.

"Talkin' New York" is done in a talking blues style, a style made famous by Guthrie, about the Greenwich Village folk scene (which Dylan pronounces, in typical contrarian fashion, as "Green-witch"). Dylan talk-sings about the New York weather—the coldest winter in seventeen years—his search for work in the Village coffeehouses, his "promotion" to bigger venues, his

BY THE WAY #3

Greenwich Village Coffeehouses

Greenwich Village is known for its coffeehouses. During the height of the folk scene, when a cup of mocha java cost sixty cents, many of these cafés were known as "basket houses," so-called because customers were encouraged to place a dollar or two in a basket on their way out or after sets—the coffeehouse equivalent of tips. The money was split among the performers. But it wasn't just folk music. There were all kinds of music being played in the Village coffeehouses: blues, bluegrass and mountain music as well as poetry readings, jazz and comedy in places such as the Rienzi, the Caricature, the Cafe Au Go Go, the Dragon's Den, the Why Not? and the Hip Bagel.

Some venues had been there for decades; others were newcomers. Unfortunately, quite a few of the more historic ones have vanished altogether. The Beats (Kerouac, Corso, Ginsberg) made the former San Remo Café (more bar than coffeehouse) at MacDougal and Bleecker famous. Boasting wooden booths, black-and-white tile floors and a pressed tin ceiling, the place was the setting of Jack Kerouac's 1958 novel *The Subterraneans*. Artists (Jackson Pollack, Willem de Kooning, Mark Rothko) favored the more austere Cedar Tavern at 82 University Place (originally located at 24 University Place, now a modern condo building). Cafe Borgia on the northeast corner of MacDougal and Bleecker was described as an old-world café. During its heyday, it attracted the Beats as well as Edward Albee, Andy Warhol, Joan Baez and James Dean. It lasted more than forty years until it closed in 2001.

Dylan played at **Café Figaro (21)** during his early days in the Village. Figaro was a single room, with old yellow copies of the French newspaper *Le Figaro*. Its most dominant feature was a loud, huge espresso machine at the back of the room. The letters of the café remain plainly visible outside its old location on the sidewalk. As we go to press, there are reports that Figaro may be revived as Figaro Café in 2021 at its original 184–86 Bleecker Street location.

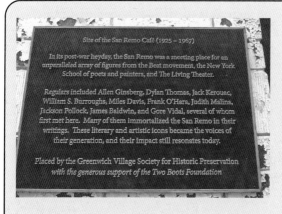

A plaque commemorates the San Remo Café, the famous Beatnik bar cum coffeehouse and hangout of everyone from Kerouac and Ginsberg to Dylan Thomas and Bob Dylan. *Photo by author.*

Dylan also frequented **Caffe Reggio (22)**, 119 MacDougal Street, and **Caffe Dante (23)**, 79–81 MacDougal Street. Caffe Reggio is one of the oldest and one of the most atmospheric coffeehouses—cozy and laid-back. It is the quintessential Village coffeehouse. (Many movies have been shot here, including Paul Mazursky's 1976 romantic comedy *Next Stop, Greenwich Village* and, more recently, the Coen brothers' *Inside Llewyn Davis*.) Handsome, old-looking paintings line the walls. Classical music plays in the background. Opened in 1927 by barber Domenico Parisi, it reportedly was the first coffeehouse to serve cappuccino in the United States. Parisi brought an espresso machine, made in 1902, from Italy with him to New York. The intimate interior also features a collection of historic artworks, including a painting by a student of Caravaggio and an antique bench that once belonged to the Medici family. In 2010, the Greenwich Village Society for Historic Preservation bestowed the café with a Village Award for being an essential part of the neighborhood.

Caffe Dante, established in 1915 and located across the street from Dylan's former townhouse, doesn't have quite the same dilapidated charm as Reggio, especially since in recent years it has reinvented itself as Dante, an elegant, upscale and sleekly modern space that features modern Italian cuisine and craft cocktails. In 2015, Australians Linden Pride and Natalie Hudson took over from the Flotta family, which had owned the coffeehouse since 1971. Four years later, in 2019, the Tales of the Cocktail Foundation (www.talesofthecocktail.org),

Caffe Reggio at 119 MacDougal Street. Caffe Reggio is one of the oldest coffeehouses in the Village. An above-street-level colorful mural captures its bohemian charm. *Photo by author.*

an annual trade conference and festival, named Dante the "World's Best Bar" and "Best American Restaurant Bar" at its Spirited Awards. Before its reinvention, though, Patti Smith was a frequent patron of Dante after her favorite coffeehouse, Café Ino (21 Bedford Street), closed. At Ino, as she notes in her lovely memoir *M Train*, she stuck to a routine, placing the same order of brown toast, olive oil and black coffee and sitting at her usual table.

During the heyday of the coffeehouse scene, so many people thronged the narrow Village streets, especially in the so-called café area from West Fourth Street to Houston Street, that the NYPD barred all nonresident vehicles unless drivers could prove they lived in the neighborhood. Despite the city's best efforts, teenagers continued to arrive. During one particularly raucous Saturday night, notes John Strausbaugh, hundreds of them marched down MacDougal Street chanting, "We shall overcome." Some were arrested for disorderly conduct. Indeed, coffeehouses were often cited as the source of tumult

Left: The extensive Caffe Reggio menu features all kinds of coffee (cappuccino, almond or hazelnut cappuccino, caffe latte, Viennese coffee, caffe mocha), paninis and sandwiches, soups and salads, as well as pastas, cheese plates, Italian pastries and even wine and beer. *Author collection.*

Right: Dante coaster. Established in 1915, Caffe Dante is one of the original Village coffeehouses, although in recent years it has been spruced up considerably. Today, it is especially known for its inventive cocktails. *Photo by author.*

and lawlessness and generally ruining or undermining the neighborhood's quality of life. According to Ronald Cohen, there were some twenty coffeehouses located in a five-block area alone.

Although not a coffeehouse, the Italian restaurant Minetta Tavern at 113 MacDougal Street is another Village fixture, famous for its food and atmosphere. A former speakeasy, it opened in 1937 and now serves a French-flavored menu with upscale prices to boot. During the folk revival, it was popular with various Village folk singers, including Tom Paxton, but the Beats also frequented it, including Allen Ginsberg, William S. Burroughs and Gregory Corso. One of the great Village characters, Joe Gould, was a regular, too. *New Yorker* writer Joseph Mitchell wrote two extensive profiles of Gould, "Professor Sea Gull" and "Joe Gould's Secret," both of which appear in his *Up in the Old Hotel* collection. A Yankee and eccentric bohemian who spoke in what Mitchell called "a twangy voice and a Harvard accent," Gould roamed the streets of the Village, cadging money and meals whenever and wherever he could and writing what he called "an oral history" of the world. His story was made into the fine 2000 film *Joe Gould's Secret* starring Stanley Tucci as Mitchell and Ian Holm as Gould.

comment about a "very great man who once said / That some people rob you with a fountain pen" (quoting here from Guthrie's "Pretty Boy Floyd"), and then leaves "New York town" for "western skies," a jokey reference to East Orange, New Jersey. The melody of "Song to Woody" was taken from Guthrie's "1913 Massacre"; Dylan's line about coming with the dust and going with the wind is from yet another Guthrie song, "Pastures of Plenty."

The cover shot of a youthful Bob Dylan (he still has his baby fat) wearing a news cap is a classic. According to Rotolo, Dylan wanted to wear a shearling jacket but couldn't afford a real one. Instead, the couple found a synthetic shearling in a Village shop on Sixth Avenue. "Bob carefully adjusted the collar, just so," notes Rotolo.

Despite the care that went into the album and John Hammond's unconditional support, Dylan's debut was something of a bust. *Bob Dylan* sold considerably less copies than Columbia had anticipated (estimates range from 2,500 to 5,000), prompting Dylan's critics to call it "Hammond's Folly," even though it cost only $402 to produce.

But its less-than-impressive sales did not faze Dylan.

He looked ahead.

The first year and a half in New York had been decisive for him. He had made a splash in the Village coffeehouses, released his first album, even performed above Fourteenth Street. Something big was about to happen. "I had a feeling of destiny and I was riding the changes....My consciousness was beginning to change, too, change and stretch."

On August 2, 1962, he made another big change: he went to the **Supreme Court building** (20) in downtown Manhattan at 111 Centre Street to become Bob Dylan legally.

The transformation was official. There was no turning back.

3
I'LL KNOW MY SONG WELL BEFORE I START SINGING

I n February 1962, Agnes "Sis" Cunningham and her husband, Gordon Friesen, founded *Broadside*, a mimeographed magazine devoted to topical songs. Despite the modesty of its operations, *Broadside* made a huge footprint within the folk community. An entire generation of singer-songwriters contributed to *Broadside*, including Tom Paxton, Phil Ochs, Arlo Guthrie, Eric Andersen, Len Chandler, Bernice Reagon, Mark Spoelstra, Richard Fariña and a then-unknown Bob Dylan. Cunningham and Friesen were among Dylan's earliest and most vigorous advocates.

Cunningham and Friesen were veterans of America's political left, Communist Party members who had been blacklisted during the McCarthy witch hunts of the 1950s. They were originally from Oklahoma and had come to New York in 1941, where they moved into the **Almanac House (24)** at 130 West Tenth Street, a folk music cooperative consisting of a loose collective of singers who specialized in topical songs (songs that comment on social or political events). Pete Seeger, Lee Hays and Millard Lampell had formed the Almanac Singers in 1940. They were soon joined by Woody Guthrie, Pete Hawes, Bess Lomax Hawes (sister of folk music collector Alan Lomax) and the Cunninghams, as well as numerous "floaters," such as Burl Ives, Earl Robinson, Tom Glazer and, occasionally, Alan Lomax.

As a center for intellectual activity as well as a crash pad for visiting folk singers, Almanac House was a true socialist collective: the members shared rent, chores and meals. In between rallies, benefits, union meetings and other bookings—and to help pay the rent—the Almanacs held hootenannies on Sunday afternoons, charging thirty-five cents at the door. Sometimes as many as sixty people would show up to hear them sing.

The rest of the time, there was work to be done. The Almanacs were always busy writing or singing something, always swapping songs and talking politics. Most famously, Guthrie wrote his autobiography, *Bound for Glory*, there. Despite the cramped quarters, the residents maintained a discreet and proper distance. "Pete and I shared the front bedroom (with a sheet hung down the middle)...being very careful not to impinge on each other and be private from each other," recalled Bess Lomax Hawes.[39]

As a group, the Almanac Singers lasted only a few years. But Seeger wanted to continue and build on the work that they created. After being discharged from the army in late 1945, he established People's Songs, an organization designed to encourage the writing and transmission of radical protest songs, and started to print a modest mimeographed bulletin that published songs and general commentary on the folk scene. He also formed People's Artists, essentially a booking agency for radical musicians. People's Songs was a template for the more commercially successful *Sing Out!* magazine, founded in 1950, as well as for *Broadside* itself. Dissatisfied with the content of *Sing Out!*—they felt it was not publishing enough topical songs—Cunningham and Friesen came up with the idea of starting their own publication, *Broadside*.

There was nothing fancy about *Broadside* or its operations. Cunningham and Friesen invited musicians to monthly meetings held in their cluttered, rent-controlled apartment in the Frederick Douglass housing project along 104th Street on the Upper West Side. These were strictly informal, down-to-earth affairs. The couple would record songs into a reel-to-reel tape recorder. Cunningham transcribed the lyrics, and Friesen jotted down commentary that would later appear in the magazine.

Broadside played a crucial role in Dylan's early development as a songwriter, publishing his songs when no one else was interested. Dylan was one of about a half dozen regulars who attended the *Broadside* meetings on the Upper West Side, even if he sometimes, in later recollections, thought the meetings took place in the Village. ("There was this place in Greenwich Village called Broadside which printed my stuff.") In any case, he was grateful for the magazine's support and eventually became a contributing editor.[40]

The debut issue of *Broadside* featured Dylan's hilariously satirical slice of 1960s paranoia, "Talkin' John Birch Paranoid Blues," also known as "Talkin' John Birch Society Blues." "Blowin' in the Wind" was published in *Broadside* before it appeared in the better-known *Sing Out!* In addition,

Dylan appeared for the first time on the cover of the folk magazine *Sing Out!* in the October–November 1962 issue. In addition to an article on the singer by Gil Turner (1933–1974), it featured the lyrics to several Dylan songs, including "Blowin' in the Wind," "Ballad of Donald White" and "Song to Woody." The terrific cover photo was taken by John Cohen (1932–2019), a musician, photographer and filmmaker who was also a founding member of the New Lost City Ramblers. *Author collection.*

Broadside published "Masters of War," "Ballad of Hollis Brown," an early version of "Don't Think Twice, It's All Right" and "The Death of Emmett Till," among other songs. Dylan appeared on the first *Broadside* album, *Broadside Ballads, Volume 1* (Folkways), under the pseudonym "Blind Boy Grunt," because he was under contract with Columbia.

Another early advocate of Dylan's songs was Gil Turner, a former Baptist preacher from Bridgeport, Connecticut, who was also the emcee of the Monday night hootenanny at Gerde's Folk City and a member of the *Broadside* editorial board. Turner also wrote for *Sing Out!* His late fall 1962 cover story for the magazine featured a profile of Dylan in which Turner called the Minnesotan "the most prolific young songwriter in America today." In the cover photo, Dylan strikes a James Dean meets Woody Guthrie pose, dragging on a cigarette with his eyes half-closed. "The songs are there," he told Turner. "They exist all by themselves just waiting for someone to write them down. I just put them down on paper. If I didn't do it," he offers with surprising modesty, "somebody else would."

During the magazine's nearly thirty-year existence, *Broadside* printed the words and music of more than one thousand songs by musicians such as Malvina Reynolds, Phil Ochs, Janis Ian and Tom Paxton. Cunningham was a composer in her own right, coauthoring with her brother Bill Cunningham the Dust Bowl classic "My Oklahoma Home" (which Bruce Springsteen included on his 2006 *We Shall Overcome: The Seeger Sessions* album). In 2000, a five-set CD, *The Best of Broadside, 1962–1988*, was released on Smithsonian Folkways. It includes an early version of "Blowin' in the Wind" by the New World Singers, as well as Dylan's "Let Me Die in My Footsteps" (with Happy Traum), "John Brown" and "Ballad of Donald White."

FREEWHEELIN'

On his second album, *The Freewheelin' Bob Dylan*, Dylan emerged as a songwriter with an original vision; the collection includes a mesmerizing combination of protest songs, astute commentaries on the burgeoning civil rights movement and lyrics that are at turns bittersweet and acerbic. The sessions began in April 1962, a mere five months after Dylan's first album was released. Significantly, all the songs on *Freewheelin'* are original compositions, even though some are based on older folk melodies.

The cover shoot of *Freewheelin'* took place along **Jones Street (25)** between Bleecker and West Fourth Streets.

Suze Rotolo's *A Freewheelin' Time*. Rotolo's 2008 memoir uses the iconic image from Dylan's second album, *The Freewheelin' Bob Dylan*, taken on a classic Village street: Jones between Bleecker and West Fourth. Sadly, she died three years later of lung cancer at age sixty-seven. *Author collection.*

Considering that it is one of the most iconic album covers of the era, it is surprising that the photo session was largely unplanned. Columbia sent a photographer over to Dylan's apartment. At the time, the album was still officially untitled, although the original working title was *Bob Dylan's Blues*. Suze Rotolo says she doesn't remember who came up with the final title, but she guesses it was either John Hammond or Dylan's manager, Albert Grossman. The spelling, on the other hand, with the dropped "g," "is all Bob," she recalls in her memoir. "He was adamant about writing down words as spoken by everyday people. He chopped off the words like a hiker hacking a path through the woods, machete in hand."[41]

According to Rotolo, Dylan chose his "rumpled" clothes for the shoot with great care. He was very deliberate about his appearance and spent an inordinate amount of time looking at himself in the mirror, "trying on one wrinkled article of clothing after another, until it all came together to look as if Bob had just gotten up and thrown something on." He had to have the right look—he had to look cool, he had to look "authentic."[42]

She was not quite as methodical: Rotolo simply put on a pullover and added another bulky knit sweater that belonged to Dylan over it to ward off the cold in the unheated apartment and to combat the freezing temperatures outside. When Columbia publicist Billy James arrived with staff photographer Don Hunstein, Hunstein took a few shots of the couple in the apartment sitting on an overstuffed armchair that they had found on the street. Because of the cramped space, Hunstein suggested they go outside. Dylan put on a thin suede jacket; Rotolo put on a green coat that she had bought in Italy. They huddled together in the wintry cold, Dylan's hands stuck deep in his pockets, and walked up and down the length of Jones Street. An instant classic was born.

PARANOIA AND CONSPIRACY BLUES

Prior to the official release of *Freewheelin'* in May 1963, Columbia sent out three hundred promotional copies to radio stations containing four songs that would not appear on the officially released version of the album: "'Talkin' John Birch Society Paranoid Blues," "Rambling Gambling Willie," "Rocks and Gravel" and "Let Me Die in My Footsteps."

As part of the album's promotion, Dylan was scheduled to appear on the *Ed Sullivan Show* on May 12. One of the *Freewheelin'* songs that Dylan planned to perform on the show was the "John Birch" song, a satiric slice of Guthriesque talking blues written from the perspective of a Birch Society member who is on the lookout for communists but ends up investigating himself. Founded in 1958 by businessman Robert W. Welch Jr., the John Birch Society was a conservative (often described as far-right) anti-communist political group that advocated limited government. It could reasonably be considered a forerunner and influence on Trumpism. (The first full-scale biography of Welch, *A Conspiratorial Life: Robert Welch, the John Birch Society, and the Revolution of American Conservatism* by Edward H. Miller, was published by the University of Chicago Press in 2022). "John Birch" is classic Dylan: sarcastic, biting, witty and dead-on funny. Considered controversial at the time, the song worried Columbia's lawyers, who were fearful of a potential libel suit and asked that the song be pulled. As a compromise of sorts, Albert Grossman convinced Dylan to drop it from the album. Ultimately, Dylan substituted "John Birch" as well as the other songs that appeared on the promo with more recent material: "Masters of War," "Talkin' World War III Blues," "Girl from the North Country" and "Bob Dylan's Dream." But he still planned to perform the song on the *Sullivan* show.

Dylan showed up early for the afternoon dress rehearsal at **Studio 50 (26)** at 1697–99 Broadway between Fifty-Third and Fifty-Fourth Streets (in 1967, it was renamed the Ed Sullivan Theater). Already there were Al Hirt, Teresa Brewer, the comedian Myron Cohen and Topo Gigio, the Italian Mouse. When Dylan rehearsed the songs, neither Sullivan nor the show's producer seemed to object. But when a CBS executive from the network's program practices department heard the "John Birch" song, Sullivan was told that Dylan could not perform it on television—it was too controversial. Instead, he suggested Dylan sing a Clancy Brothers song. "It just didn't make sense to me to sing a Clancy Brothers song on nationwide TV at that time," Dylan said years later in a radio interview. Rotolo says Dylan was furious— he called her from the rehearsal studio "in a fit." He refused to back down and walked off the show.[43]

TIN PAN ALLEY

Tin Pan Alley is an odd term that originally referred to a nondescript street in Manhattan located along Twenty-Eighth Street between Fifth and Sixth Avenues where the nuts-and-bolts business of American popular music flourished during the late nineteenth century and the first few decades of the twentieth century.

By the turn of the twentieth century, New York had become the undisputed world capital of music publishing. The publishers, which included M. Witmark & Sons, Charles H. Harris and Shapiro and Bernstein, were based mostly in what was then the heart of the Theater District, in Union Square along Fourteenth Street. Before long, though, they followed the theaters as they moved farther uptown to Twenty-Eighth Street and finally to Midtown. (Robert Snyder captures the intoxicating atmosphere of the era in his evocative social history, *The Voice of the City*, published by Ivan R. Dee in 2000.)

Music publishers congregated around this particular corner of Manhattan; the frenzied sound of tinny pianos being played at the same time reportedly led to the coining of its unusual name. A journalist for the *New York Herald* by the name of Monroe Rosenfeld first used the term *Tin Pan Alley* in a series of articles that he wrote for the paper. Writers gathered in cramped, tiny cubicles, scribbling down lyrics or whatever thoughts came into their heads. Each cubicle had its own upright piano. The Tin Pan Alley way was songwriting by collective, a give-and-take method that produced the optimal result: a hit song. The pianos were played simultaneously as writers moved from cubicle to cubicle, agilely changing a word to a lyric here or adding one there. In the days before air-conditioning, every window was open to bring in much-needed fresh air. The cacophony of different tunes being played all at once reminded Rosenfeld of tin pans being clashed together.

Many of the most influential music publishers got their start at Tin Pan Alley as salesmen. Before entering the music business, some had sold water filters, others corsets and still others neckties and buttons. To them, a song was just another item to be retailed. And being the natural salesmen that they were, they took to their new profession with ease and a great deal of gusto.

The songwriters of Tin Pan Alley kept their ears close to the ground. They read the newspapers daily, borrowing themes and subject matter from the headlines to use in their songs. They were also on the lookout for trendy catch phrases—anything to give their songs a contemporary cachet, something that would be easy for the average person to remember.

Tin Pan Alley brought together many different styles of music: blues, jazz, ragtime, music hall. The songs were sophisticated but also street smart. More important, they were democratic: the songwriters wrote the songs for and about the people. The songs were idiomatic and used everyday slang. Economical—they were nothing if not exemplars of brevity—the songwriters turned the clichés of the day into sparkling wit.

With the exception of Hoagy Carmichael and Cole Porter, who hailed from the American Midwest, and Johnny Mercer from Georgia, most of the second generation of Tin Pan Alley songwriters were New York Jews. They included Harold Arlen, Irving Berlin, Dorothy Fields, George and Ira Gershwin, Larry Hart, Jerome Kern and Richard Rodgers. Their songs were so successful that they would become popular standards. And virtually all of these standards were love songs—love songs written by professional songwriters for professional performers.

Dylan was the antithesis of Tin Pan Alley. He had little use for the formulaic love songs that were the building blocks—the DNA— of the alley canon. "Who needs them?" he once asked an interviewer. "Not you, not me." At one point, he even famously bragged, "Tin Pan Alley is gone. I put an end to it." And that boast is more or less true. He set in motion a transformation of the songwriting business, inspiring a generation of singer-songwriters who had no need for Tin Pan Alley's assembly line of catchy but conventional melodies and undemanding lyrics. Whether consciously or unconsciously, Dylan upended the old order—at least for a while. Today, another kind of Tin Pan Alley—if by Tin Pan Alley we mean songs written by professional songwriters for professional singers—resides in Nashville along that city's Music Row.[44]

After Dylan signed the contract with Columbia, Hammond arranged for him to meet Lou Levy at Leeds Music Publishing on the Upper West Side. Dylan was naïve to the ways of the music industry, and he signed a contract with Leeds Music giving the company the right to publish his songs for an advance of $100. In December 2020, Universal Music Publishing Company signed a deal to purchase Dylan's entire songwriting catalog for an estimated $300 million, according to media reports (the actual price was not officially disclosed).

Levy took the young songwriter to Jack Dempsey's at Fifty-Eighth and Broadway to celebrate the occasion and introduced Dylan to Dempsey, the heavyweight boxing champion, who strolled up and down the aisles of his legendary restaurant like a lion protecting his cubs, playing the role of the amiable host, greeting guests, signing autographs and posing for photographs. The restaurant, which opened in 1935 and closed in 1974, was a popular hangout. Dempsey's was pricey—only patrons with deep pockets could afford to dine there—so it meant something that Levy wanted to show off his new prospect. When Levy told Dempsey that Leeds would be publishing Dylan's songs, Dempsey sized up the scrawny Minnesotan with a "Good luck to you, kid" and then moved on to the next table.[45]

Albert Grossman was not impressed with the Leeds contract. When Grossman became Dylan's manager in the summer of 1962, he made sure his client got a better deal. Grossman arranged for Dylan to be released from the contract and signed with Tin Pan Alley publisher **Witmark and Sons (27)**, at 488 Madison Avenue at Fifty-First Street, for a $1,000 advance. Dylan began regularly visiting the Witmark office to record demo versions of his songs in order for them to be transcribed for copyright purposes and used as sheet music.

Witmark was a prestigious music publishing company founded by Isidore Witmark, a Prussian immigrant, in 1885. It published the work of George M. Cohan and Victor Herbert, musical giants in their day. Dylan was the first folk singer the company signed.[46]

Dylan recorded demos at Witmark, on the fifth floor of the *Look* magazine building, as it was then called, in a cramped studio just six feet wide and eight feet long. Most of those recordings appear on *The Witmark*

Demos, Bootleg Series Vol. 9. Released in 2010, it consists of forty-seven tracks, fifteen of which were previously unreleased. Despite his youth, Dylan sounds much older than his actual age. At turns humorous and acerbic, upbeat and confident, he is a young man in a hurry ("I have too much to get done," he sings at one point) and already world-weary ("I know I ain't no prophet and I ain't no prophet's son"), his driving guitar style accentuating the urgency of his vocals.

The Witmark Demos also provide a peek at a transitional moment in popular music history. Dylan was both the writer and the publisher of the songs. It was the end of one era—Tin Pan Alley—and the beginning of another—the singer-songwriter era, with Dylan leading the way. Indeed, within a decade, the singer-songwriter movement would reach its apotheosis, as the songs of Joni Mitchell, Neil Young, James Taylor, Jackson Browne, Cat Stevens, Carole King and Paul Simon, to cite some of the most prominent members of the first wave, attained levels of popularity and status that set the stage for subsequent generations to build on.

"BLOWIN' IN THE WIND"

Freewheelin' opens with the anthemic "Blowin' in the Wind," Dylan's first commercially successful song—and one of his most enduring compositions.

Dylan first played "Blowin' in the Wind" backstage at a Monday night hootenanny at Gerde's Folk City. "I got a song you should hear, man," said Dylan, nervously, to emcee Gil Turner. "Sure thing, Bob," Turner replied. Another folk singer, David Blue, recalled that Dylan sang the song "with great passion." A crowd gathered round; they were stunned into silence. Turner was so impressed with the song that he asked Dylan to teach it to him on the spot. He wanted to sing it on stage. Dylan wrote down the words, and Turner taped the lyrics onto a mike stand on the stage. "Ladies and gentle-men," he announced to the audience, "I'd like to sing a new song by one of our great songwriters. It's hot off the pencil, and here it goes."[47]

Before Dylan recorded the song, his manager provided an acetate to arranger and record producer Milt Okun, who worked with various folk acts at the time, including the Brothers Four, the Chad Mitchell Trio and Peter, Paul and Mary. Everyone, it seemed, wanted to record it.

The first time the song appeared on an album was on *The Chad Mitchell Trio in Action*, released in March 1963. Less than six months later, Peter,

Paul and Mary recorded it. Their version went (almost) to the top of the charts, reaching as high as number two in August 1963: it sold 320,000 copies in eight days and became the fastest-selling single in Warner Bros.' history up to that point. In total, it has sold more than 2,000,000 copies and, according to Dylan scholar Michael Gray, has been recorded by various artists at least 375 times.[48]

During the song's meteoric rise, Dylan sang it himself in the Village clubs. When he performed it at Gerde's, he prefaced it by saying, "This here ain't a protest song or anything like that, 'cause I don't write protest songs....I'm just writing it as something to be said, for somebody, by somebody." He also sang it on radio programs. It was one of three songs he performed on the *Broadside* reunion show in May 1962 on WBAI-FM. The lyrics were published the following month in *Sing Out!* magazine. Dylan didn't actually record it until July, when he went into Columbia's Studio A during one of the *Freewheelin'* sessions. "I wrote it for the moment, ya know," Dylan once said. "I remember running into Peter [Yarrow] in the street." "Man," Yarrow told Dylan, "you're going to make $5,000."[49]

Although released as a single, "Blowin' in the Wind" is the last song on Peter, Paul and Mary's album *In the Wind*. As an informal thank-you for recording it, Dylan wrote a long, stream-of-conscience poem that celebrates and commemorates the Village coffeehouse scene, especially the Gaslight, in the sleeve notes. The Gaslight, he writes, was "a heat pipe poundin subterranean coffee house" that was "buried beneath the middle a MacDougal Street." Just two years after arriving in New York, Dylan already was waxing nostalgic about a time that must have seemed far in the past. Everybody at the Gaslight was close, he said ("Yuh had t' be"). It was the kind of place where you were watching out for one another "an find out about ourselves." He makes reference to the Gaslight's various characters: Paul Stookey, the emcee who was then known as Noel; Dave Van Ronk; and Hugh "Wavy Gravy" Romney. Dylan had first met Peter Yarrow in Minneapolis, when Yarrow was traveling through town as the guitarist for a dance troupe, and he knew Mary Travers from his earliest days in the Village. In the poem, Yarrow's beard is "only about half grown," while Travers's hair "was down almost t' her waist then." Those days are gone, he laments, "An they'll not never come again."[50]

Dylan borrowed the melody for "Blowin' in the Wind" from an old freedom song, a spiritual, called "No More Auction Block (Many Thousands Gone)" that originated in Canada and was sung by black freedmen who fled there after Britain abolished slavery in 1833. The only known performance of

Dylan performing "Auction Block" was recorded at the Gaslight in October 1962; it appears on the *Gaslight 1962* recording.

"Blowin' in the Wind" is at least partly responsible for one of the great songs of the civil rights era, Sam Cooke's "A Change Is Gonna Come." Cooke was moved that a white man could have written such a powerful anti-racist and pro-freedom protest song. Inspired partially by Dylan as well as by Martin Luther King Jr.'s "I Have a Dream" speech at the August 1963 March on Washington, and angered by a racist incident he experienced when he and his entourage were turned away from a whites-only motel in Shreveport, Louisiana, Cooke resolved to write his own protest song. "A Change Is Gonna Come" was recorded in late January 1964 and initially released in mid-February 1964. It wasn't until after Cooke's death, though, in December 1964, when it was released as a single, that it gained traction and was quickly embraced by civil rights activists. Regina King's powerful 2020 film *One Night in Miami* takes some creative liberties when Malcolm X (Kingsley Ben-Adir) puts Dylan's song on the turntable and asks Cooke (Leslie Odom Jr.) why it took "a white boy from Minnesota" to effectively capture the spirit of the civil rights movement, thereby suggesting a stronger and more direct link existed between Dylan's song and "Change." Dramatically speaking, though, it works.

HIS OWN WORDS

Dylan says that he cannot remember when it first occurred to him to write his own songs. He wanted to write the kind of songs that he wanted to sing—he had no interest in singing the commercial songs then heard on the radio. And the songs that he most wanted to write largely hung on a folk song skeleton. "My life had never been the same since I'd first heard Woody on a record player in Minneapolis a few years earlier. When I first heard him it was like a million megaton bomb had dropped." Once he was settled in the Village, he began memorizing poems to challenge his mind. "I began cramming my brain with all kinds of deep poems." Dylan believed that memorizing poems such as Lord Byron's "Don Juan" and Samuel Taylor Coleridge's "Kubla Khan" helped him with his own writing.[51]

Once he started to write his own songs, Dylan developed his skills at an astonishing pace; his songwriting progressed by leaps and bounds. He began experimenting with entirely new forms of songwriting—and the intoxicating atmosphere of being in New York stoked his creative juices. He strove not just for success but for greatness. He has said that he was not entirely satisfied with "Blowin' in the Wind"—he wanted to create something that was singular and yet distinctly his own. He told the *New York Times*'s Robert Shelton in 1966, "I was actually most afraid of death in those first years around New York...because I still hadn't written what I had wanted to."

As Dylan's career progressed, his songwriting turned increasingly toward topical themes. *Freewheelin'* contains several classics of the genre: most famously "Blowin' in the Wind," but also "Masters of War" and "Oxford Town," indications of the direction that his career would follow. A ferocious anti-war song, "Masters of War" is just as powerful and relevant today as it was when it was first written. Thirty years after he recorded it, Dylan performed an acoustic rendition at a concert in Hiroshima; he has also updated its lyrics to comment on the Iraq War.

The first political song Dylan composed, "The Death of Emmett Till," in 1962, was written for CORE, the Congress of Racial Equality. Suze Rotolo was a part-time volunteer at CORE's 38 Park Row office in downtown Manhattan, across from City Hall Park (its headquarters today is at 817 Broadway). "The violence in the South was terrifying; all of us working in the New York office were in a constant state of tension," she recalled. She arranged to have Dylan perform the song at a benefit concert for the organization on February 23, 1962.

Partly in response to Rotolo's influence, Dylan continued to write political songs. With the success of "Blowin' in the Wind," Dylan was being hailed, much to his chagrin, as America's great white conscience. Joan Baez, for one, was "knocked out" by "Emmett Till," and when Judy Collins saw the lyrics of "Blowin' in the Wind" in the pages of *Sing Out!*, she wrote Dylan a fan letter, her first.[52]

By responding to the times, Dylan had become, unwittingly, the voice of a generation—a title that he became increasingly uncomfortable with as his career progressed.

Following Tradition

Dylan used traditional songs as a template. "From folksongs, I learned the language...by singing them and knowing them and remembering them.... English ballads, Scottish ballads, I see them in images....It goes deeper than just myself singing it," Dylan told *Gargoyle* magazine. By the time he wrote "A Hard Rain," he had internalized the old ballads—from both the Old

World and the New World.[53] From his earliest days in New York, he studied the works of John and Alan Lomax, Francis James Child and Cecil Sharp.

Dylan borrowed the melody and song structure from the traditional Scots ballad "Lord Randall" for "A Hard Rain's A-Gonna Fall." Both songs use the question-and-answer skeletal framework. In the original ballad, a conversation takes place between a young man and his mother as he slowly reveals to her that he is dying from poison. Whereas in the traditional ballad, the dialogue asks, "Oh where have you been, Lord Randal, my son?" Dylan changes it to "Oh where have you been, my blue-eyed son?"

Dylan mixed images of innocence with those of devastation that superseded the Cold War crisis. He transformed "Lord Randall" into a modern-day parable on politics, the threat of war and the very real possibility of annihilation. These were not the kind of topics usually covered by popular songs.

Dylan has said that he wrote the song in September 1962 in the basement apartment of Chip Monck, the Village Gate's lighting engineer. "I'd write songs at people's houses, people's apartments, wherever I was." But Tom Paxton offers a contradictory recollection. Paxton says that he and Dylan were in a tiny room above the Gaslight where they played poker and hung out. Dylan was typing a poem on Hugh "Wavy Gravy" Romney's typewriter. "One day I walked in and there was Bob with this portable typewriter. He was pounding away and I asked him what it was. He said it was 'just a poem.' I said, 'Why don't you sing it?'"[54]

In the liner notes for *Freewheelin'*, Dylan goes so far as to call "A Hard Rain" "a desperate kind of song. Every line in it is actually the start of a whole song. But when I wrote it, I thought I wouldn't have enough time alive to write all those songs so I put all I could into this one." In April 1963, he played in Chicago for the first time, where he performed at the Bear, a North Side folk club that Dylan's friend Howard Alk opened earlier in the year. Dylan's manager, Albert Grossman, who had met Alk in New York, booked Dylan into the club and arranged, according to Michael Gray, for Dylan to do two unpaid shows "for the exposure." Dylan was introduced as the "folk artist Bobby Dylan." While in town, he recorded an hour-long radio and performance interview with Studs Terkel on WFMT-FM. On the show, he tried to explain the significance of "Hard Rain": "I remember sitting up all night with some people, some place, and I wanted to get the most down that I knew about into one song as I possibly could....It's not atomic rain, though," he told Terkel. "Some people think that. It's just a hard rain, not the fall out rain, it isn't that at all. The hard rain that's gonna fall is in the last verse, where I say the 'pellets of poison are flooding us all,' I mean all the lies that people are told on their radios and in the newspapers, trying to take people's brains away, all the lies I consider poison....I just mean some sort of end that's just gotta happen." The repetition was intentional. "I kept repeating things I feared," he said.[55]

"A Hard Rain's A-Gonna Fall" is the first of an ambitious cycle of songs that includes "Gates of Eden" and "Desolation Row," visionary pieces that transcended the limits of popular songcraft. Dylan introduced "A Hard Rain" at **Carnegie Hall (28)** on September 22, 1962, when he was part of a multi-artist hootenanny lineup sponsored by *Sing Out!* magazine. Others on the bill that evening included Pete Seeger, Scots singer Matt McGinn, the New World Singers and Bernice Johnson (better known today as Bernice Johnson Reagon). Each artist was limited to ten minutes in which he or she could play no more than three songs, which posed a problem for Dylan, because "Hard Rain" was at least seven minutes long. Even though the crowd roared in approval, a frustrated Dylan left the stage after singing the one song, disappointed by both the restrictions imposed on him and his performance.

THE TOWN HALL

On April 12, 1963, a month before *Freewheelin'* was released, Dylan appeared at a concert at the **Town Hall (29)**, 123 West Forty-Third Street. Known for its outstanding acoustics, the Town Hall was built by the League for Political Education, a politically liberal group that fought for passage of the Nineteenth Amendment and wanted to establish a venue where everyone was welcome. The architectural firm McKim, Mead, and White used basic democratic principles in its design: all seats offer unobstructed views.

The Town Hall concert established Dylan as a major voice in folk music. And yet, despite his burgeoning reputation, the hall was only two-thirds full. Columbia recorded the concert with the intention of releasing it later as a live album to be called *Bob Dylan in Concert*. But for whatever reason, the project was scrapped. Dylan premiered a number of songs that night, songs that he either never performed again or never recorded, including "Who Killed Davey Moore?" A topical song, "Davey Moore" refers to a featherweight championship boxing match that took place on March 22, 1963, in Los Angeles between Moore and Cuban "Sugar" Ramos. When Ramos knocked Moore out in the tenth round, Moore fell into a coma;

"Harold Leventhal presents Bob Dylan at Town Hall, April 12, 1963." Dylan performed at the historic Town Hall a month before his second album, *The Freewheelin' Bob Dylan*, was released. Note that one of the reviewers praises Dylan as "One of the most compelling blues singers ever recorded." Leventhal (1919–2005) managed some of the biggest names on the folk scene, including the Weavers, Woody Guthrie, Pete Seeger, Judy Collins, Theodore Bikel, Arlo Guthrie, Joan Baez, Mary Travers and Tom Paxton. *Author collection.*

he died three days later. Less than three weeks after the bout, Dylan was performing the song, even though he still had a few kinks to iron out. Here Dylan played the role of the broadside balladeer, reporting and commenting on the news in song and getting it out—in those relatively slow-moving, pre-digital days—in front of the public as quickly as possible. He filched the melody from the nursery rhyme "Who Killed Cock Robin?"

Dylan sang the first performance of "Boots of Spanish Leather" at the Town Hall that night. He introduced other songs there too, including "With God on Our Side," which he would record four months later and was based on Dominic Behan's song "The Patriot Game." (Dominic was the brother of Brendan.) A powerful and darkly sarcastic anti-war song ("And the land that I live in / Has God on its side"), it contains some of Dylan's most incendiary lyrics.

For the Town Hall encore, Dylan made a rather unusual choice: for the first and only time he recited one of his poems in public, "Last Thoughts on Woody Guthrie"—straight from the page (the rustling of paper can be heard on the recorded version). Although Guthrie was still alive—he didn't die until October 1967—"Last Thoughts on Woody Guthrie" is a farewell from one songwriter to another. It is written in a free-form, stream-of-consciousness style, very Whitmanesque, an intoxicating flood of words, images and ideas, as Dylan expresses occasional moments of self-doubt ("You say to yourself just what am I doin' / On this road I'm walkin', on this trail I'm turnin'") before concluding on a defiant note, finding a heroic gesture in the most mundane and ordinary pursuits of everyday life.

Dylan wrote his autobiography several times—fictional biography is perhaps a more accurate way of describing it—during these early years. Another of his prose poems, "My Life in a Stolen Moment," was included in the concert's program notes. It is part fact, part fiction—and big part pure invention. The piece opens with references to Minnesota, to the open pit and movie houses and bars of Hibbing, to his recollections of growing up there—all true enough—and to his various trips across the country (his version of Guthrie's "hard travelling"), his arrival in wintry New York, more travels and a brief nod to his influences. Then it comes full circle, returning to Hibbing.

The poem recalls his first trip to New York, where he "Walked a winter's line from the Lower East Side to Gerde's Folk City." He pays homage to his many heroes, Guthrie as well as Big Joe Williams, and he somehow manages in a few lines to make references to various cultural flashpoints: the classic blues song "Stagger Lee" ("the bull-dog's bark"), James Joyce's *Finnegans Wake* ("an' mile cow's moo") and Hank Williams ("An' the train whistle's moan").

CARNEGIE HALL

Six months after the Town Hall show, Dylan moved even farther uptown with a solo concert at Carnegie Hall. "We all sensed a sea change," writes Suze Rotolo about the concert, "and it was exhilarating." The show took place between the fifth and final sessions for *The Times They Are A-Changin'*, his third album, which was released early in 1964. Dylan began with the debut performance of the title track from the album, which had been recorded several days earlier. He also performed the visionary "Lay Down Your Weary Tune," one of the outtakes from the *Times* sessions. Although considered one of his more obscure songs, a few critics have written about it extensively: Dylan scholar Michael Gray devoted an entire chapter to the song in his *Song & Dance Man III: The Art of Bob Dylan*.

A recent trip back home to Minnesota led to "North Country Blues," a bleak ballad that uses a blues structure and is written from the perspective of a miner's widow. In his brief introduction to the song, Dylan said, "I'm sure you all know about the coal mining countries in West Virginia and southern

Pennsylvania. This is a song about the ore country. I wrote this in a woman's words." He sang a protest song, "Only a Pawn in Their Game," that he had first performed at a rally on July 6 in Greenwood, Mississippi, three weeks after the assassination of the secretary of the National Association for the Advancement of Colored People (NAACP), Medgar Evers.

Dylan's parents were in the audience that night; he had sent them tickets and even paid for their airfare to New York. Prior to the concert, Columbia publicist Billy James had arranged for Dylan to meet with a reporter from *Newsweek* magazine. According to Clinton Heylin, Dylan sensed that the reporter, whom Heylin identifies as Andrea Svedberg, was digging for dirt. The word was that she didn't buy Dylan's story and wanted to discover who the real Bob Dylan was. She became frustrated by what she perceived to be Dylan's lack of cooperation. During the actual interview, says Heylin, Dylan "grew irate, and stormed off into the night." He returned in time to perform for his parents.[56]

But the cat was out of the bag, and Dylan's North Country roots—and his true ethnic heritage—were exposed. The uncredited article that ran in *Newsweek* a week after the concert notes that Dylan "shrouds his past in contradictions," and that he "is the elder son of a Hibbing, Minn., appliance dealer named Abe Zimmerman and, as Bobby Zimmerman, he attended Hibbing High School, then briefly the University of Minnesota." The reporter wonders why Dylan bothers to deny his past: "Perhaps he feels it would spoil the image he works so hard to cultivate—with his dress, with his talk, with the deliberately atrocious grammar and pronunciation in his songs."[57]

The article raises the issue of whether Dylan actually wrote his most famous song, "Blowin' in the Wind," and mentions an ill-founded rumor that a Millburn, New Jersey high school student named Lorre Wyatt composed it. In the January 1964 issue of *Sing Out!*, editor Irwin Silber sets the record straight. He refers to a letter that Wyatt sent to the magazine in which he states that he wrote a song called "Freedom Is Blowing in the Wind" *before* he heard Dylan's song and that both the words and the melody were entirely different.

Dylan was deeply embarrassed, if not angered, by the *Newsweek* article. He felt especially bad for his parents—the article made him look like a phony and a liar. Already suspicious of the press, he closed ranks and began to rely solely on his inner circle for support. His problematic relationship with the media would grow increasingly combative and secretive over the next few years.

BY THE WAY #4

Mary Travers

The female third of Peter, Paul and Mary, Mary Travers was born in Louisville, Kentucky, but moved with her family to New York when she was a child. Thus, unlike the vast majority of the folk singers who traveled great distances to come to the Village, she was *from* the Village: she went to school there and grew up there and at one point lived across the street from the Gaslight on MacDougal. She attended Elisabeth Irwin High School (the lower and middle schools are located at 272 Sixth Avenue at Bleecker Street), a private progressive high school that was originally known as the Little Red School House.

Because her innate shyness made performing difficult, Travers initially considered folk singing as a mere hobby. But Peter Yarrow convinced her to give it a chance. Within a short period of time, PPM became one of the most popular folk groups in the world and among the most prominent interpreters of Dylan's songs. To mainstream America, Peter Yarrow and Paul Stookey, with their goatees and mustaches, accompanied by the blond, good-looking Mary, epitomized Greenwich Village. They were America's quintessential folk singers.

Mary Travers died on September 16, 2009. A few months later, her life was commemorated at the Riverside Church on the Upper West Side in a four-hour memorial. A capacity crowd of two thousand people attended. The speakers included Pete Seeger, Judy Collins and Theodore Bikel, with video testimonials from Bill Clinton, Bill Cosby, Gloria Steinem and Harry Belafonte. Her former bandmates, Peter Yarrow and Paul Stookey, performed. Dylan, however, did not attend.

4
REVOLUTION IN THE AIR

ylan matured quickly as a writer. He was churning out songs at a
remarkable rate. During 1962 alone, he wrote around fifty songs. "I
could do that then," he reflected years later, "because the process was
new to me." The world was changing faster than people could keep up with
it, and Dylan reflected the frenetic pace. Yet by the simple act of expressing
himself, he seemed to offend a lot of people.[58]

Between the Town Hall concert in April 1963 and the Carnegie
Hall concert in October 1963, Dylan performed at a civil rights rally in
Greenwood, Mississippi; the Newport Folk Festival; the Forest Hills tennis
stadium with Joan Baez; and the March on Washington. All the while he
continued to soak up all kinds of intellectual stimulation in New York. He
saw plays by Jean Genet and Bertolt Brecht as he continued to consider what
kind of songs he wanted to write. The world that he saw portrayed on stage
was chaotic and meaningless—it reflected his still unformed feelings. He
knew that the songs that he would write would be similar in tone and texture
and theme. "They wouldn't conform to modern ideas."

Endlessly curious and hungry for knowledge, Dylan continued his self-
education, reading extensively. He spent many hours at the **New York
Public Library (30)**, Fifth Avenue at Forty-Second Street. Overwhelmed
by its grandeur, by its sheer majesty, Dylan considered it "a building that
radiates triumph and glory when you walk inside." Maybe he was hoping
some of that radiance would rub off on him. He frequented an upstairs
reading room, where he viewed newspaper articles on microfilm from the

mid-1850s to learn what daily life was like back then. He had a particular fascination with Abraham Lincoln and the Civil War era, but he also read from the works of Tacitus, Machiavelli, Milton and Pushkin. He also devoured volume after volume in the private libraries of friends: books on philosophy; novels by Gogol, Balzac, Maupassant, Hugo and Dickens; the poetry of Byron, Shelley, Longfellow and Poe.[59]

In the folk music world, 1963 can be viewed as the year of the hootenanny. The public's appetite for folk music seemed to be insatiable. ABC broadcast a program called, appropriately enough, *Hootenanny*; at least one radio station, WCPO in Cincinnati, began playing folk music seven days a week; more than two hundred folk albums were released in the United States that year, and at least two dozen magazines catering to folk were published, including Robert Shelton's *Hootenanny*, which featured a bimonthly column called "Blowin' in the Wind" by none other than Bob Dylan. Dylan was allowed to write whatever he wanted—by then, people were becoming accustomed to his idiosyncratic spelling. For his efforts, he was paid a modest seventy-five dollars. (Both the column and the magazine were short-lived.)

DYLAN ON BRECHT

Suze Rotolo continued to be a major influence. Rotolo had many cultural interests, which she enjoyed sharing with Dylan. They caught shows at the **Village Vanguard (31)** at 178 Seventh Avenue South, went to avant-garde and foreign movies; listened to records at friends' apartments; read the classic and modern poets, from Dickinson to Millay; and saw off-Broadway theater including Leroi Jones's *The Dutchman* at the Cherry Lane Theatre at 38–42 Commerce Street in the Village and the Living Theatre's *The Brig*. In addition to her volunteer work at CORE, Rotolo also did odd jobs at the theater. In the late spring of 1963, she began work on a production of *Brecht on Brecht* at the now-demolished **Sheridan Square Playhouse (32)**, 99 Seventh Avenue South. The same production had a run at the Theater de Lys at 121 Christopher Street—it has since been renamed the Lucille Lortel Theatre—with Lotte Lenya as the headliner. But this production, says Rotolo, was "bare bones." *Brecht on Brecht* was a theatrical collage of Brecht's poems, songs, plays and letters put together by the Hungarian writer and director George Tabori.

Dylan was impressed by the Brecht production, especially by the lyricism of Brecht's work. One song in particular captured his imagination: "The

Black Freighter," otherwise known as "Pirate Jenny" from Brecht and Kurt Weill's musical *The Threepenny Opera*. "Pirate Jenny" left him "breathless," partly because of its raw intensity and partly because of the honesty of its emotions. "Pirate Jenny" is written from the perspective of a scullery maid who seethes with anger because she feels she is unappreciated by the "gentlemen" guests of a rundown hotel. She counts the days until redemption arrives in the form of a "ghostly" ship called the *Black Freighter*, which features a skull on its prow. She holds the power of life and death in her hands. As the song concludes, she chooses the latter, unapologetically.

It is neither a protest song nor a love song. It exists in a world all unto itself. Returning to his Village apartment, Dylan listened to a recording of the original off-Broadway production over and over again. One line in particular—"you could hear a foghorn miles away"—reminded Dylan of the foghorns on Lake Superior back in Duluth, the town where he was born.

Dylan meticulously and methodically deconstructed the song in order to figure out to his own satisfaction just how, and why, it made such a powerful impact on him. He experienced something of an epiphany: he realized that the songs that he wanted to write didn't exist—at least, they were not the kinds of songs played on the radio—and that if he wanted to hear them, he would have to write them himself. Brecht's compositions offered a blueprint for Dylan to follow.

Dylan was well aware that writing songs—good songs, that is—is not an easy thing to do. "You want to write songs that are bigger than life." When he started writing his own songs, he used the folk tradition as a template. "I changed words around and added something of my own here and there.… You could write twenty or more songs off…one melody by slightly altering it. I could slip in verses or lines from old spirituals or blues. That was okay; others did it all the time." In his view, it didn't really matter the origins of a song. What mattered was "where it takes you."

The New School

Suze Rotolo also exposed Dylan to the art world. Her favorite contemporary artist at the time was Red Grooms, a multimedia artist who created pop art that reflected the chaos of urban life. Grooms soon became a favorite of Dylan's, too. Nashville born, Grooms moved to New York in 1956 to attend the New School for Social Research. Grooms combined painting and sculpture that featured colorful caricatures of modern street life. Dylan felt a connection to this work, seeing a visual equivalent in Grooms's paintings to the folk songs that he himself admired so much. "[Grooms] incorporated every living thing into something and made it scream—everything side by side created equal….Subconsciously, I was wondering if it was possible to write songs like that."[60]

Through all these early influences—the traditional ballads, Woody Guthrie, songs heard in the Village coffeehouses, the theater, the art world and the zeitgeist of New York itself—Dylan internalized what he learned and turned it all into something entirely new.

CHANGING TIMES

The mood in the Village was changing along with that of the rest of the country. Dylan felt it, felt the urgency and tension in the streets and reflected this urgency and tension in his songs. "There was music in the cafés at night / And revolution in the air," he wrote years later in "Tangled Up in Blue."

The Times They Are A-Changin' was recorded between August and October 1963 and released in January 1964. Consisting of ten original compositions performed solo on acoustic guitar and harmonica, it is both a prophetic statement and an accurate assessment of its time. It was released just two months after the assassination of John F. Kennedy, and it seemed to capture the palpable feeling of change that was in the air. In fact, Dylan called the material on it "finger-pointin' songs" and "call to action" songs. "I'm going through changes," he said. "Need some more finger-pointin' songs in it, 'cause that's where my head's at right now. I don't think when I write. I just react and put it down on paper."[61]

All the songs on the album were written in New York, and New York shaped the songs in ways both simple and profound. Many were inspired by listening to various performers in New York City cafés and coffeehouses. "I'd never have written any of them—or sung them the way I did—if I hadn't been sitting around listening to performers in New York cafes and the talk in all the dingy parlors," Dylan later admitted. "When I got to New York it was obvious that something was going on—folk music—and I did my best to learn and play it."[62] In a 1978 interview, Dylan said that New York "was a great place for me to learn and to meet others who were on similar journeys….I was given some direction there, but I took it, too."[63]

For a time, musicians from all corners of the globe seemed to converge at the corner of Bleecker and MacDougal Streets. And why not? The rents were cheap—"Thirty dollars pays your rent / On Bleecker Street," Simon and Garfunkel once sang—and the company was stimulating. Suze Rotolo remembers Dylan sitting in one of the outdoor coffeehouses on Bleecker Street, writing all day. At night, he would jot his thoughts down on a yellow pad or compose on a typewriter "and go at it until he gave out. He was always working on something—always."

To Dylan, New York was a drug, an intellectual stimulant that served as an endless stream of inspiration. It was the sound of the streets, the sound of open windows where snippets of conversation floated in the dusky glow of an early dawn; he took it on himself to get it all down on paper and, ultimately, on record.

The songs on *The Times They Are A-Changin'* are strongly influenced by balladry. Although the prophetic title song coincided with the assassination of JFK, it reflected the burgeoning civil rights movement and the first serious rumblings against the Vietnam War. "This was definitely a song with a purpose," said Dylan. "I knew exactly what I wanted to say and for whom I wanted to say it to. You know, it was influenced by the Irish and Scottish ballads....Come all ye bold highwaymen, come all ye miners, come all ye tender-hearted maidens. I wanted to write a big song, some kind of theme song...with short concise verses that piled up on each in a hypnotic way."[64]

The stark and evocative Dust Bowl era–like photograph on the cover, taken by Barry Feinstein, the husband of Mary Travers (they later divorced), signifies the somberness of the material. A solemn-looking Dylan strikes a Guthriesque pose: he wears a work shirt open at the collar, his eyes downcast, his lips slightly pursed, with a serious expression on his face as if the entire world were resting on his young shoulders.

The album's liner notes featured a long prose-poem by Dylan called "11 Outlined Epitaphs," which starts on the back cover and continues on the inside. Written in a loose, Beat-like style, it includes numerous autobiographical references, similar to his earlier prose-poem "My Life in a Stolen Moment."

In "Epitaphs," Dylan concludes that men are, after all, just men and that Guthrie himself is just a man, not a god. He would elaborate further on this topic during an interview with Nat Hentoff in the October 24, 1964 issue of the *New Yorker*. In that interview, Dylan discussed how the press was exposing him—undoubtedly referring to the *Newsweek* exposé—even though the media had no way of knowing that he felt he was exposing himself every time he went onstage. He stated that he refused to cooperate with a press that sought to portray him as "the boy next door" or answer what he considered ridiculous questions.

Dylan refers to Duluth in "Epitaphs" as "the town that I was born in." The associations, though, are vague; he writes that it "holds no memories but for the honkin' foghorns / the rainy mist / the rocky cliffs." On the other hand, he has strong memories of his childhood town, Hibbing, which left him with "legacy visions." But even then he viewed his hometown through less than rose-colored glasses; he was ready to embrace "what I left / an' lovin' it—for I learned by now / never t' expect / what it cannot give me." His hardheaded approach led to his conclusion that Woody Guthrie would be his "last idol."

In the poem, Dylan waxes nostalgic about his early days in New York—despite being in the city for only a few years. He wonders if cockroaches still crawl in Dave Van Ronk and Terri Thal's kitchen on Fifteenth Street. He ends with a long list of his many heroes, a wildly diverse and quite remarkable bunch. Is it coincidental that one of his heroes is François Villon? In addition to being a poet, Villon was famous for being a thief and a vagabond as well as a connoisseur of the bohemian lifestyle. Dylan concludes with a line from another Frenchman, François Truffaut's film *Shoot the Piano Player*, a favorite of his at the time: "Music, man, that's where it's at."

SPEAKING OUT LOUD

Allen Ginsberg once commented that Dylan "pissed people off for not being a nice trained seal." One incident epitomizes this thought: a few weeks before the release of *Times*, on December 13, 1963, Dylan accepted the Tom Paine Award in the Grand Ballroom of the **Americana Hotel (33)** at 811 Seventh Avenue between Fifty-Second and Fifty-Third Streets. The tallest hotel in the world when it was built, the site is now the location of the ultramodern Sheraton New York Hotel & Towers.[65]

Dylan was flying high. He had two albums under his belt and was anticipating the imminent release of a third one. He had performed at two of the finest concert halls in New York City, the Town Hall and Carnegie Hall, and now an important civil rights organization wished to express its appreciation of his work by honoring him with its annual award. All he had to do was show up and give a speech. For someone with a reputation as a brilliant wordsmith, it should have been smooth sailing.

Easier said than done.

The National Emergency Civil Liberties Committee (NECLC), better known as the Emergency Civil Liberties Committee (ECLC), was founded in 1951. Since 1958, the organization had presented the annual Tom Paine Award in recognition of distinguished service for civil liberty. In 1963, the board determined that Dylan was worthy of receiving it (actually, it was the idea of civil rights activist Clark Foreman).

When Dylan got up on stage to receive the award, he looked out at the audience and then at his colleagues on the podium, which included the author James Baldwin neatly attired in a suit and tie. Dylan was clearly uncomfortable in the august setting and felt out of place. "I haven't got any guitar," he nervously began. Riffing a line from "My Back Pages," which he hadn't recorded yet, he said, "It's took me a long time to get young and now I consider myself young. And I'm proud of it." He repeated the sentence. He then proceeded to insult the members of the audience who had gathered to celebrate his achievements during a remarkable year. Worse, he suggested that he and John F. Kennedy's assassin, Lee Harvey Oswald, might have something in common. "I saw some of myself in him." The crowd was shocked and responded with boos and hisses. "You can boo, but booing's got nothing to do with it," he said, inadvertently egging them on. He left the stage amid more boos and a scattering of applause.[66] (Decades later, he would revisit the Kennedy assassination in his 2020 single "Murder Most Foul," which appeared on *Rough and Rowdy Ways*, his thirty-ninth studio album.)[67]

The committee depended on contributions for survival, and the format of the planned evening called for solicitation pledges to begin immediately after Dylan finished talking. Not surprisingly, few people in the audience felt generous enough to write a check. Afterward, Foreman estimated that Dylan's little speech cost the committee a cool $6,000 in lost contributions. At least one member resigned in disgust.

Dylan felt compelled to explain his behavior to the people who had tried to honor him. In a letter to the ECLC, he made a clumsy attempt at an apology, but it fell woefully short and failed to explain his motivations. Today, it's still not clear what led Dylan to say what he did that evening. Dylan wrote in the letter that he does not claim "to know any kind of truth." As far as the reference to Oswald, Dylan says he was speaking of the times, not the deed. "The deed speaks for itself."

In the letter Dylan also tried to describe the effect that New York had on him. "I would not be doing what I'm doing today if I hadn't come to New

York. I was given my direction from new york. I was fed in new york. I was beaten down by new york and I was picked up by new york. I was made to keep going on by new york." He was, he concluded, "reborn in New York."

Dylan's Other Side

Like the country in general, Dylan's personal life was in flux. In March 1964, he broke up with Suze Rotolo, although they had been drifting apart for some time. She resented being considered Dylan's "chick," a mere appendage. "I did not want to be a string on Bob Dylan's guitar," she says. She had moved out of the Fourth Street apartment in August 1963. There were other complications: Dylan had started a relationship with Joan Baez. They had performed together at the Monterey Folk Festival in May 1963, and Dylan had accompanied Baez on her tour of the Northeast.

He continued to work despite the personal upheavals. *Another Side of Bob Dylan*, released in the summer of 1964, was a turning point. A transitional album as well as an artistic breakthrough, it was recorded in one boozy evening session. Dylan walked into Columbia's Studio A on Seventh Avenue around 7:00 p.m. on June 9 with several bottles of Beaujolais and half a dozen friends, including Ramblin' Jack Elliott and the writer Nat Hentoff, and left at 1:30 the next morning. Most of the songs had been written during a one-week span in the late spring of 1964 while he was in Vernilya, Greece, after completing his first British tour.

On the album jacket, which features a New York street scene, Dylan looks appropriately cool, distant and aloof. He wears a dark suede jacket and jeans, his left leg propped up, his left elbow resting on his left thigh, his right hand on his hip. If the Dylan on *The Times They Are A-Changin'* looked as if he had walked out of a Dust Bowl photograph, this Dylan looks as hip and detached as a young Jack Kerouac.

But what made the album different were the songs. Although the sound hadn't changed much from the previous album, it seemed fuller and denser (Dylan added the piano); the lyrical content had changed, too. What is strikingly absent on the album are the "finger-pointin'" songs. According to Dylan, "There aren't any finger- pointing songs in here. Now a lot of people are doing finger-pointing songs. Me, I don't want to write for people anymore. You know, be a spokesman....From now on, I want to write from inside me."[68]

Indeed, aside from the surreal "Chimes of Freedom," there is nary a protest song among them. Instead, Dylan created a series of highly personal songs, including love songs ("All I Really Want to Do," which would become a hit for Sonny and Cher, and "To Ramona"), and a blues song with honky-tonk roots ("Black Crow Blues"). There is a New York song, "Spanish Harlem Incident," about a "gypsy gal" in Harlem, and a talking blues song, "I Shall Be Free No. 10." The album also features the raucous "Motorpsycho Nitemare" (in which Dylan name-drops the titles of several classic films, including *Psycho* and *La Dolce Vita*) and several anti-love songs ("I Don't Believe You," "It Ain't Me Babe" and the caustic and bitter "Ballad in Plain D," about his breakup with Rotolo). It also contains "My Back Pages," which became a hit for the Byrds.

The album defied expectations. Dylan's songs were deeply personal at a time when politics was a growing national concern. And the love songs he was writing were not the kind of songs that the music factories were churning out. Dylan's songs were heartfelt, angry and honest—perhaps too honest for some people. Disregarding the conventions usually associated with love songs, he upended platitudes and custom. It looked like Dylan was trying to kill the love song—or at least give it a mortal blow.

"My Back Pages" is Dylan's personal statement, circa 1964. He turns his back on his former self, the preachy protest singer, and the protest songs that the world had come to expect from him. Instead, he embraces a younger version of himself ("I was so much older then / I'm younger than that now"). His voice has a youthful tone, too, more joyful and less strident. Dylan may have been ready for the world to hear this new version, but did his audience want to listen?

PHILHARMONIC CONCERT

Dylan spent the summer and early autumn catching up with an old flame (Bonnie Beecher from Minnesota) and a few new ones (an off-and-on relationship with Baez and a burgeoning one with a model named Sara Lownds, who would eventually become his wife). On October 31, 1964, Dylan performed at **Philharmonic Hall (34)**, at 132 West Sixty-Fifth Street. It took many years for the concert to appear on a recording—the performance was released in March 2004 as *Bob Dylan Live 1964: The Bootleg Series, Vol. 6, Concert at Philharmonic Hall.*

The Philharmonic Hall had opened two years earlier as part of Lincoln Center. Later called Avery Fisher Hall at Lincoln Center and, in 2015, renamed David Geffen Hall, when it opened it was considered the most prestigious venue in the United States. Thus, in a few scant years, Dylan had traveled from Greenwich Village coffeehouses to the Town Hall, to Carnegie Hall and now to the Philharmonic. In the audience were two Beat icons, Allen Ginsberg and Gregory Corso. As one critic noted, the concert was "the last strains of a self-aware New York bohemia before it became mass marketed."[69]

Dylan sang seventeen songs that night, including three with Joan Baez and one encore. By now, many in the audience knew a fair number of the songs, although a few songs were brand new. At first, the crowd didn't quite know what to make of the new ones. Dylan was moving in a direction that his audience could not anticipate. But the songs he sang that Halloween night were not performed in a vacuum. Dylan was keenly aware of what was going on in the world.

It was a chaotic and frightening time. The civil rights movement had turned violent with the murders in Mississippi of the civil rights workers James Chaney, Andrew Goodman and Michael Schwerner. Despite the turmoil, or perhaps because of it, President Lyndon Johnson had managed to push through Congress the historic Civil Rights Bill in July, a goal of the martyred John F. Kennedy. The war in Vietnam was escalating. In mid-October 1964, China had detonated its first atomic bomb, which caught Americans, and the rest of the world, off guard.

Dylan first walked onstage unannounced. Beginning with "The Times They Are A-Changin'," he offered irreverent and self-deprecating introductions, making light of the songs and their inherent earnestness. Toward the end of the first half of the performance, he forgot the opening line of his next song and asked the audience to help him out. They were only too happy to oblige. He sang for the first time some of the songs from his forthcoming *Bringing It All Back Home*. He prefaced "Gates of Eden" by calling it "A Sacrilegious Lullaby in D Minor." He also introduced "It's Alright Ma (I'm Only Bleeding)" as the audience listened intently. After a fifteen-minute intermission, the second half of the show was devoted to familiar songs, mostly from *Freewheelin'* and *Times* as well as three duets and an encore with Baez. At one point wearing a plaid Glengarry cap, perhaps as a nod to her half-Scottish heritage (her mother, Joan Bridge, was born in Edinburgh), Baez sang "Mama, You Been on My Mind," "With God on Our Side" and "It Ain't Me, Babe." She sang solo on "Silver Dagger" with Dylan accompanying her on the harmonica. The night ended with the encore performance of "All I Really Want to Do."

Robert Shelton's review in the *New York Times* called the show "an engrossing program," as Dylan "made the best of his small voice. His diction was clear and his singing was frequently moving and evocative." In fact, Dylan was fast becoming a critical darling. Within a few years, he would be referred to as "Homer in denim" (the *Guardian*) and "Brecht of the jukebox" (the *Village Voice*).[70]

Dylan wrote a new prose-poem to accompany the program booklet. Titled "Advice for Geraldine on Her Miscellaneous Birthday," it consists of a series of mostly cynical, and quite funny, comments on identity and art: "do Not create anything, it will be misunderstood," said one. Another suggested that "when asked t' give your real name…never give it." These humorous ramblings and slogans are reminiscent in style and tone of "Subterranean Homesick Blues," which he would record early the next year.

"JUST LET ME BE ME"

As Dylan's professional life was changing, so too was his personal life. The fame was getting to him; the city was getting to be too crazy. Slowly, Dylan was turning away from the New York that had nurtured him to spend more time upstate. He felt that, psychologically, he needed to keep his distance from the city. Increasingly, he used the Bearsville, New York home of his manager, Albert Grossman, "as a refuge between concerts." He admitted to Nat Hentoff that "being noticed can be a weight. So I disappear a lot." He was treated fine in the Village ("People don't pay attention to me"). But he lamented that strangers thought they knew him and, worse, knew everything about him. "I was still running when I came to New York," he said, before adding, "Just because you're free to move doesn't mean you're free." Rotolo has commented on how fame changed him. "He was given permission to do or say whatever he wanted," she observed.[71]

The pressure was evident even before the Philharmonic concert. Earlier that year, in the January 20, 1964 issue of *Broadside*, Dylan wrote an open letter to editor "Sis" Cunningham and her husband, Gordon Friesen, that smacked of desperation. It is a brutally honest dispatch on fame and its aftereffects. "I am now famous," he writes, and "it snuck up on me / and pulverized me." He admits that sometimes he likes being recognized and signing autographs. But other times he considers it a dishonest act. "I am livin in a contradiction." He feels overwhelmed by all the attention ("an what am I anyway? Some kind a messiah walkin around…?") and undeserving of it ("hell no I'm no").[72]

In the letter, Dylan confesses that he is lonely ("a lonely person with money is still a lonely person") and that his mind can't keep up with his thoughts ("my mind sometimes runs like a roll of toilet paper / an I hate like hell to see it unravel an unwind"). He complains about his filthy—and cold—apartment ("the damn heat goes off at ten/and dont come on til ten…that's mornin wise"). The plaster is falling off, the floor is rotting. As he is typing the letter he listens to Pete Seeger—who he calls a saint—singing "Guantanamera."

To an outsider, it seemed like Bob Dylan had the world in his hands. His fans loved him, critics praised him and his popularity was growing beyond Manhattan. But he had to pay a price for his success, and he wasn't sure if he could afford it. Everyone wanted a piece of him.

Dylan was many things to many people. To some, he was a prophet; to others, a silver-tongued poet with a guitar; and to still others, the incarnation of Woody Guthrie in 1960s garb. Shelton called him "the brilliant singing poet laureate of young America." But Dylan was growing weary of all the masks he had to wear in public, all the personas he had assumed over the years; he was drained by the demands placed on him.

Dylan decided he didn't want to be anyone else's idea of Bob Dylan anymore. "Just let me be me," he pleaded.

5

MYSTERY TRAMPS AND NAPOLEONS IN RAGS

Although 1965 began on a professional high note—the recording sessions for *Bringing It All Back Home* started in mid-January—Dylan's personal life was, once again, in shambles.

After he moved out of the Fourth Street apartment in the summer of 1963, he began spending more time with Joan Baez. He had started the affair with Baez in May 1963, when she appeared on stage with him to sing "With God on Our Side" at the Monterey Folk Festival. Dylan stayed with Baez after the festival ended, enjoying the sun and sea breezes near her Carmel, California home.

Baez invited Dylan along as her guest on her summer tour. Later that summer, on August 28, he sang with her at the Lincoln Memorial during the March on Washington. When they were in New York at the same time, they stayed at the **Hotel Earle (35)** at 103 Waverly Place (Dylan Thomas had also stayed there), across the street from Washington Square Park. Dylan was familiar with the hotel, having spent a short time there when he first arrived in New York. The Earle was little more than a fleabag hotel then (in her 1975 song "Diamonds and Rust," Baez refers to Dylan as "the unwashed phenomenon / the original vagabond" and the Earle as "that crummy hotel / over Washington Square"), but today it is the decidedly more upscale Washington Square Hotel, a handsome boutique establishment. (The Hotel Earle's reputation went up and down over the years. When Ernest Hemingway stayed there in 1918, he called it a "very nice Hotel." It opened in 1902 and was renamed the Washington Square Hotel in 1986.)

Even after Rotolo moved out and in with her sister Carla, Dylan and Rotolo still saw each other. It was all very complicated. They broke up for good in March 1964, after Rotolo had an abortion. The decision, she says, was a difficult one, but it was a joint one.

That fall and winter, Dylan spent a great deal of time trying to escape from what critic Luc Sante has called "the burden of himself." If *Another Side of Bob Dylan* provoked anger from Dylan's hardcore folk fans, his fifth album, *Bringing It All Back Home*, left many dumbfounded, shaking their collective heads at this latest musical work that he had foisted on an unsuspecting public. This new album was almost unclassifiable. *Another Side of Bob Dylan* had paved the way for this so-called new Dylan. His work grew increasingly surreal, personal and ambiguous, becoming further removed from the protest songs that had made him famous.[73]

A BEAT SENSIBILITY

Dylan's connection to the Beats goes back to Dinkytown, where he first read Kerouac's *On the Road, Mexico City Blues* and *Visions of Gerard*, as well as Ginsberg's "Howl" and Ferlinghetti's "Coney Island of the Mind." "I came out of the wilderness," Dylan said, "and just naturally fell in with the beat scene." Greil Marcus, for one, believes that Dylan's "Like a Rolling Stone" owes more to "Howl" "than to any song."[74] Greenwich Village was a bigger version of Dinkytown. No wonder it appealed to him.

In Dinkytown as in the Village, Beats and folk singers overlapped. If they didn't always follow the same circles, there was still no way of avoiding one another, bumping into one another in clubs, cafés and coffeehouses. The writing of Kerouac, Ginsberg, Burroughs, Ferlinghetti and Corso made as significant an impact on Dylan's artistic evolution as Elvis Presley and early rock and roll. Dylan, the Jewish boy from a small midwestern town, identified with Kerouac, the French Canadian Catholic from a small industrial New England town who also came to New York as an outsider. Kerouac-like symbolism and imagery surface in Dylan's songs. Dylan clearly admired the freeverse association of the Beats and the looseness and fluidity of their language.

Dylan's connection to Ginsberg is more tangible and dates to November 1963, when journalist Al Aronowitz introduced the singer and the poet at Ted Wilentz's apartment above the **Eighth Street Bookshop (36)** at 32 West Eighth Street. (In 1965, it moved across the street to a larger space, at 17 West Eighth Street, a five-story townhouse with three floors' worth of books.)

The Eighth Street Bookshop was owned by Ted and his brother Eli (Dylan historian Sean Wilentz is the son of Eli). The party that November night was a welcome-home celebration for Ginsberg and his companion, Peter Orlovsky, after their return from a trip to India. Both men were avid supporters of the bookshop. The Wilentz brothers published some of Ginsberg's early work, and Orlovsky had once worked there as a janitor. The party was the same day as Dylan's disastrous speech at the Americana Hotel. But rather than discussing Dylan's unsettling performance, Ginsberg and Dylan talked about poetry and politics, forging the beginnings of a friendship.

The Eighth Street Bookshop called itself "Greenwich Village's Famous Bookshop." It carried the city's largest selection of poetry and stocked Sartre and Camus before their works were fashionable. More significantly, it was *the* literary gathering place at the time, a throwback to the pre–World War I era, when Mabel Dodge presided over the most famous literary salon in American history at her Fifth Avenue apartment, bringing together the movers and shakers of New York to engage in wide-ranging conversations on art, politics and society.

Consequently, the Eighth Street Bookshop was more than just a mere bookshop. It was also a post office drop for writers, a makeshift employment agency, a place where people (usually struggling writers in between royalty checks) could borrow a few bucks. The Wilentz brothers hired poets to stock shelves and sweep the floors. LeRoi Jones, before he changed his name to Amiri Baraka, worked there, as did, for a short time, his wife, poet Hettie Jones, sorting bills and checks. During its heyday, regular clientele included Edward Albee, Uta Hagen, Susan Sontag, Irving Howe, Joseph Campbell, Michael Harrington, Joseph Mitchell, W.H. Auden, e.e. cummings, Marianne Moore and Kerouac and Corso. The Eighth Street Bookshop was also a publisher, printing books under the Corinth Books imprint, including the early works of Ginsberg, Gary Snyder, Philip Whalen and Diane DiPrima.

When fire gutted the store in 1976 and it nearly burned to the ground, some of the city's poets, writers and editors held a fundraising party, at which a distraught Ginsberg composed an extemporaneous poem on the spot, "The Burning of the Eighth Street Bookstore." "It was really pretty good," recalls the poet and editor Harvey Shapiro.[75]

Dylan refers to Ginsberg and another one of his heroes, Hank Williams, in the liner notes for *Bringing It All Back Home*, noting that the fact that Ginsberg was not chosen to read poetry at President Lyndon Johnson's inauguration "boggles my mind." The album is heavily indebted to the Beats. Dylan had absorbed a Beat sensibility into his music as his lyrics grew more sophisticated and complex, cryptic and allusive, strange and mysterious, merging poetry with song. Dylan also shared Ginsberg's surrealist imagination in songs like "Subterranean Homesick Blues." Later, on *Highway 61 Revisited* and *Blood on the Tracks*, he would take the Beat framework—its language and its cadences—and apply them to pop songs.

Ginsberg admired Dylan's work from the start. The poet once said that when he first heard Dylan—a friend played him "Masters of War"—he wept. "It was a sense that the torch had been passed to another generation."

BRINGING IT HOME

Dylan went into the Columbia studio for *Bringing It All Back Home* in January 1965. By incorporating a level of lyrical sophistication unheard of in popular music, Dylan laid the foundation for contemporary as well as future generations of musicians to build on, from Joni Mitchell to Elvis Costello to the Decemberists. The music was a wild pastiche of rock, folk and blues that didn't sound like anything on the radio.

Dylan had become increasingly impatient and frustrated with the framework of the folk genre. Where does poetry end and song begin?, he asked. "I've been getting freer in the songs that I write," Dylan told Nat Hentoff, "but I still feel confined. That's why I write a lot of poetry." "Gates of Eden" reflects this urge to slip the bonds of folk songwriting. The corrosive "It's Alright, Ma (I'm Only Bleeding)" was written in Woodstock in Upstate New York, and the farewell song, "It's All Over Now, Baby Blue," can be interpreted as an adieu to a relationship or as a rejection of his former self—perhaps both. Dylan was tired of being confined by the restrictions of the folk genre and the attitudes of the folk establishment, which wanted him to conform to specific ideas of what kind of music he should be making.[76]

He wrote most of the songs on the album between November 1964 and January 1965. Like *Another Side of Bob Dylan*, *Bringing It All Back Home* was recorded very quickly—over three consecutive days. It is divided into an electric side and an acoustic side—as if Dylan wasn't sure which musical direction to follow.

The album kicks off with the subversive "Subterranean Home Sick Blues" about the absurdities of contemporary life and punctuated by traces of paranoia ("Keep a clean nose / Watch the plain clothes"); words of advice ("Don't follow leaders"); and phrases that would soon become part of the counterculture parlance ("You don't need a weatherman / To know which way the wind blows"). With its basements and parking meters, the song sounds as though it could only have been written in New York. Side 2 begins with "Mr. Tambourine Man," which the Byrds would take to the top of the charts. Dylan has said that the song was inspired by a seventeen-inch Turkish tambourine, actually a large Turkish frame drum, with a sheepskin head and jangly bells that belonged to session guitarist Bruce Langhorne. Langhorne had bought it at Izzy Young's Folklore Center in the Village. Dylan knew Langhorne from when they had both worked together on a Carolyn Hester album, and Langhorne played on *Freewheelin'* and *Bringing It All Back Home*, including "Mr. Tambourine Man." Dylan recalled that Langhorne's tambourine was "as big as a wagonwheel" and that this vision of him playing a huge tambourine "just stuck in my mind." But others see the influence of the French poet Arthur Rimbaud on Dylan. In particular, Richard Thomas in *Why Bob Dylan Matters* finds a parallel between Dylan's visionary lyrics and Rimbaud's equally vivid and dreamlike words, especially in his poem "The Drunken Boat."

Reaction to the album varied. The members of the Old Guard were upset. *Sing Out!*, in particular, lashed out at Dylan. "It's a pity and a frustration," wrote editor Irwin Silber, "for if ever the world was in need of the clear and uncompromising anger and love of the poet it is now."[77]

Dylan responded with a metaphorical shrug. He had already moved on.

BACK TO THE STUDIO

Dylan started working in New York on *Highway 61 Revisited* in June 1965. A few days after the late-July Newport Folk Festival fiasco—when Dylan famously plugged in his guitar and started a musical revolution—he returned to Studio A to record the remainder of the album's songs, including "Desolation Row" and "Positively 4th Street." The new album announced beyond any doubt that Dylan was going in a new direction. He recorded with a full rock band behind him and created, in the confines of the studio, some of the best-known and highly praised songs of the rock era.

Introduced at Newport, "Like a Rolling Stone" is a vengeful put-down and one of the most famous songs in rock—as well as one of Dylan's most popular. (Music critic Greil Marcus considers it the greatest pop single ever and wrote an entire book about it, *Like a Rolling Stone: Bob Dylan at the*

Crossroads.) "I'd never written anything like that before and it suddenly came to me that that was what I should do." Originally, it was ten pages long "about my steady hatred directed at some point that was honest. In the end it wasn't hatred, it was telling someone something they didn't know." He never thought of it as a song until he sat at the piano at "a little cabin in Woodstock" that he was renting from Peter Yarrow's mother. With the crucial line "How does it feel?" he had the beginning of a song.[78]

Another ferocious put-down, "Ballad of a Thin Man," was Dylan's response to a persistent journalist who was always asking questions. At various times, the enigmatic figure of Mr. Jones was said to be a reporter at the *Village Voice*, a former critic at *Melody Maker* and even an intern at *Time* magazine. "There were a lot of Mr. Joneses at that time," Dylan later said.[79]

Several other songs were composed either in Woodstock or in New York City. The title track was written while Dylan and his girlfriend, Sara Lownds, were living in Yarrow's small cabin in Woodstock. "We had come up from New York," said Dylan, "and I had about three days off to get some stuff together." It is an example of the ultimate tall tale, a type of folk blues, and is as idiosyncratic a piece of popular music as has ever been created. Essentially, it is Dylan's version of the story of Abraham put to the patter of a 1960s hipster.

The dreamlike "Just Like Tom Thumb's Blues" is full of literary references, from Malcolm Lowry's *Under the Volcano* to Edgar Allan Poe to Arthur Rimbaud. It takes place somewhere on the metaphorical road where invariably strange things happen. But the protagonist can only take so much and, in a nice geographical twist, looks forward to returning to the normalcy of the city ("I'm going back to New York City / I do believe I've had enough").

Dylan reportedly wrote "Desolation Row" in the back of a New York City taxicab. An eleven-minute epic, it contains gypsies and historical figures, including the Hunchback of Notre Dame, T.S. Eliot, Ezra Pound, Victor Hugo and Albert Einstein. "Positively 4th Street" was recorded during the *Highway 61* sessions but does not appear on the album. Instead, it was released as a follow-up single to "Like a Rolling Stone."

Dylan's use of language in *Highway 61 Revisited* changed how people wrote popular songs. Out were the moon/June lyrics of previous generations. In were ambiguity and complexity. He had addressed the issue of songwriting a few years earlier in the liner notes for *Freewheelin'*. "Unlike most of the songs nowadays being written uptown in Tin Pan Alley, that's where most of the folk songs come from nowadays, this"—referring to "Bob Dylan's Blues"—

The Brill Building on Broadway at Forty-Ninth Street was built in 1931. During its heyday, it served as the center of pop music songwriting when countless composers worked there. A partial list includes Burt Bachrach, Hal David, Neil Diamond, the husband-and-wife team of Gerry Goffin and Carole King, Howard Greenfield, Ellie Greenwich, Jerry Leiber and Mike Stoller, Barry Mann, Laura Nyro, Doc Pomus, Neil Sedaka and Cynthia Weil. *Photo by author.*

"wasn't written up there—this was written somewhere down in the United States." The remark was meant to be a slight against the **Brill Building (37)** sound, which had its headquarters at 1619 Broadway. During the late 1950s and early 1960s—the pre-Beatles, pre-Dylan era—about a dozen or so mostly Jewish songwriters composed popular songs that captured the imagination of teenagers around the world. Essentially, the Brill Building sound was the baby boomer equivalent of Tin Pan Alley.[80]

Dylan's songwriting skills intimidated even the best of the Brill Building composers. Gerry Goffin, who with then-wife Carole King, wrote such 1960s classics as "Will You Love Me Tomorrow," "One Fine Day" and "Up on the Roof," was astonished at the complexity of Dylan's work: "I wish we had tried more to write some songs that—really meant something," said Goffin. "Dylan managed to do something that not one of us was able to do: put poetry in rock 'n' roll….We said we gotta grow up, we gotta start writing better songs now."[81]

HOTEL CHELSEA

After Rotolo left the Fourth Street apartment, Dylan spent less and less time in New York and more time upstate. When he was in the city, he usually stayed either at his manager's apartment on Gramercy Park West or in Room 211, a one-bedroom suite, at the **Hotel Chelsea (38)** at 222 West Twenty-Third Street with Sara Lownds, whom he would wed in a private civil ceremony on November 22, 1965. (He reportedly at various times also lived in Room 215 and Room 225.)

The slightly out-of-focus cover shot of Dylan on the cover of *Blonde on Blonde* (rock's first double album) by Jerrold Schatzberg was taken near the Hotel Chelsea, and some of the songs on the album were written there. The thirteen-minute "Sad Eyed Lady of the Lowlands," Dylan's paean to Sara, was said to be inspired by the time the couple spent at the hotel, but whether it was written there, as the lyrics to the 1975 song "Sara" attest ("Staying up for days in the Chelsea Hotel / Writing 'Sad Eyed Lady of the Lowlands' for you," Dylan sings), is another thing. Clinton Heylin believes that most of the song was written not at the Chelsea but rather in Tennessee; although Dylan began recording *Blonde on Blonde* in Studio A in October, by February 1966, the recording sessions had moved to Nashville to Columbia's Music Row Studios.

Other literary endeavors were created at the Chelsea, including Arthur C. Clarke's *2001: A Space Odyssey* and William S. Burroughs's *The Third Mind*. Madonna, a former resident in the 1980s, returned to Room 822 in 1992 to shoot photographs for her book *Sex*. Joseph O'Neill's 2008 novel *Netherland* was partly set here.

In any case, Dylan appreciated the Hotel Chelsea and its eccentricity and felt its anything-goes atmosphere would get his creative juices flowing again (he wrote "Visions of Johanna" there). Built in 1883 as an apartment

Opposite: Hotel Chelsea. Built in the 1880s, the famous hotel has been the home to many writers, musicians, actors and artists. In addition to Dylan, other musicians have included Chet Baker, Tom Waits, Patti Smith, Jim Morrison, Iggy Pop, Virgil Thomson, John Cale, Marianne Faithfull, Robbie Robertson, Leonard Cohen, Rufus Wainwright and Madonna. *Photo by author.*

Above: *All Seeing Eye* painting on rooftop at Hotel Chelsea. Among the most prominent residents of the two-story, pyramid-shaped rooftop penthouse was indie filmmaker Shirley Clarke. Clarke hosted numerous get-togethers here. *Photo by author.*

cooperative, the twelve-story Hotel Chelsea began operating as a hotel in 1905. When I wrote the first edition of this book, in 2011, half of its 240 rooms belonged to guests, the other half to residents. Residents and guests lived in usually comfortable proximity to one another. None of the rooms were alike. Over the years, residents have included Brendan Behan, Eugene O'Neill, Simone de Beauvoir, Leonard Cohen, Allen Ginsberg, Jimi Hendrix, Willem de Kooning, Jasper Johns, Janis Joplin, Arthur Miller, Joni Mitchell, Jean-Paul Sartre, Harry Smith, Patti Smith, Mark Twain, Tom Waits and Tennessee Williams. Arthur C. Clarke wrote *2001: A Space Odyssey* here; Jack Kerouac wrote *On the Road*. It is famous for other reasons, too: in 1953, the Welsh poet Dylan Thomas was staying here when he died after a drunken night at the White Horse Tavern. More notoriously, on October 12, 1978, Sex Pistols' guitarist Sid Vicious stabbed Nancy Spungen to death here.

Several movies have been made about or feature the Chelsea. Andy Warhol and Paul Morrissey directed *Chelsea Girls* in 1966, an underground film about Warhol's Factory regulars. The 2009 documentary *Chelsea on the Rocks* by Abel Ferrara features interviews with some of its most famous—and infamous—guests, including William S. Burroughs, Andy Warhol and Dennis Hopper. In 2002, actor Ethan Hawke directed *Chelsea Walls*, a fictional portrait of five artists during one day at the hotel.

During its mid-aught years, the decor, clientele, and overall atmosphere felt as if they belonged in a Jim Jarmusch film, while the long, dim hallways were reminiscent of a scene out of the Coen brothers' *Barton Fink*. An oversized black-and-white photograph of Jack Nicholson in *The Shining* hung on a hallway. Much of the artwork—whether mounted on the hallways, painted directly on the walls and stairwells or hanging in the lobby—was creepy in a surprisingly appealing way, including the bizarre papier-mâché "Woman on a Swing" and "Chelsea Dogs," an oil-and-wood construction by South African artist Roy Carruthers. Although the room that Sid Vicious and Nancy Spungen stayed in has been destroyed and parts of it incorporated into other apartments since her murder, eerie reminders of it popped up here and there. Artist Robert Lambert's portrait of Sid Vicious, "Sid the Kid," hung in the hallway outside Room 515: Sid, his head tilted to the side, wears blue jeans and a white sleeveless T-shirt and has a knife in his right hand and a syringe in his left. The name *Nancy* appears in the lower left-hand corner. For years, artist-in-residence Lambert ate and slept in a tiny room in the Chelsea. "I like living in my studio," he told visitors. Inside his room/studio were various examples of his work: portraits of Stanley Bard, the former manager of the hotel; Andy Warhol; Albert Einstein; and Leonard Cohen.

Dylan and Sara moved out of the hotel "maybe a year before" the Warhol film *Chelsea Girls* was released in 1966, returning north to Woodstock. "When *Chelsea Girls* came out," says Dylan, "it was all over for the Chelsea Hotel. You might as well have burned it down."[82]

Even the Chelsea is not immune to changing times. In 2010, this last outpost of bohemia, as some have called it, was put up for sale. The owners stopped accepting long-term residents, a radical departure from previous policy. Lambert moved out. Chelsea veterans fear that the famous hotel might be turned into some kind of bloodless bohemian theme destination ("See where Sid killed Nancy!"). Renovation has been proceeding, albeit very slowly on a stop-and-go basis. As of this writing, approximately fifty residents remain in the hotel. At press time, the reopening of the hotel was announced by late 2021. To be continued....

The Silver-Haired King on His Chrome Horse

When he wasn't with his wife, Sara, in Upstate New York, Dylan continued to savor the city nightlife. Andy Warhol's Factory studio, then located on the fifth floor of 231 East Forty-Seventh Street, was a favorite hangout. (The building no longer exists.) In 1967, Warhol moved his headquarters downtown to the **Decker Building (39)** at 33 Union Square West. (Built in 1892, it was in the lobby of this building on June 3, 1968, that a deranged fan, Valerie Solanas, shot Warhol three times. He survived but was never quite the same.) In 1973, Warhol moved the location again—to 860 Broadway.

The Factory was a popular hangout for hip New Yorkers as well as assorted hangers-on. Among the musicians who used it as a meeting place were Lou Reed, Nico, Mick Jagger and Brian Jones. Reed's song "Walk on the Wild Side" refers to various members of the Factory crowd, while some believe Dylan's "Like a Rolling Stone," a modern-day fairy tale about a rich girl down on her luck, may be modeled after Edie Sedgwick, the blonde model and occasional actress who became famous for being famous.

Dylan met Sedgwick at the Kettle of Fish on MacDougal Street in late 1964, when he was still living at the Chelsea Hotel. Shortly thereafter, Sedgwick linked up with Andy Warhol; by March 1965, she was starring in her first Factory film, *Vinyl*. She appeared in other Warhol films, including *Space*, *Restaurant*, *Poor Little Rich Girl*, *Kitchen*, *Horse and Beauty #2*. Filmmaker D.A. Pennebaker, the director of the classic Dylan documentary *Dont Look Back*, shot a lot of footage of Sedgwick, although she does not appear in the film. According to Dylan lore, Sedgwick is the woman portrayed in "Just Like a Woman," "Leopard Skin Pill-Box Hat" and "Stuck Inside of Mobile with the Memphis Blues Again"; she may even be the blond of *Blonde on Blonde*. Not everyone is convinced, though: "There's no evidence—and no real grounds to suppose," Michael Gray writes, "that Dylan and Edie had any personal relationship at all, let alone a significant one."[83]

Sedgwick wasn't the only celebrity to appear in Warhol's films. In 1965, Dylan agreed to do a "screen test" for Warhol for one of the artist's underground films. Consisting of a series of short films, they were meant to be the celluloid equivalent of paintings. Altogether, Warhol created nearly five hundred of these short films.

Sedgwick died of a barbiturate overdose in Santa Barbara in 1971 at the age of twenty-eight. The film *Factory Girl*, released in 2006, stars Sienna Miller as Sedgwick, Guy Pearce as Warhol, Patrick Wilson as John Cale, Brian Bell as Lou Reed, Meredith Ostrom as Nico and Hayden Christiansen as the Dylanesque character, although the filmmakers—Dylan had threatened to sue—could not use his name. Instead, he is given the enigmatic moniker of the Musician.

Within walking distance of the downtown Factory location was **Max's Kansas City (40)** at 213 Park Avenue South, a combination bar and restaurant that was a popular hangout for Warhol and his entourage as well as a coterie of numerous actors, musicians, artists and sycophants. The owner, Mickey Ruskin, had a soft spot for creative folk. In addition to Dylan, regulars included artist Robert Rauschenberg, poet and photographer Gerald Malanga, Dylan's right-hand man Bobby Neuwirth and Nico and members of the New York Dolls. With the exception of the white walls, everything at Max's was red, including its tablecloths and napkins. In the back room was a round table where Warhol and his court reigned like latter-day princes and princesses.

BEATLES AND SPIDERS

During this chaotic period, while juggling his complicated personal life and an increasingly demanding touring schedule, Dylan still managed to find the time to meet the Beatles while they were staying at the **Delmonico Hotel (41)** at 502 Park Avenue at Fifty-Ninth Street on the leg of their first American tour. It was here, on August 28, 1964, where Dylan famously introduced them to the pleasures of marijuana. (The Delmonico is now called the Trump Park Avenue and is a private luxury condominium owned by Donald Trump.) That same month, Joan Baez accompanied Dylan to meet with Robert Markel, an editor at Macmillan, then located in the Village. (It is now at Fifth Avenue and Twenty-Third Street.) Markel was interested in publishing Dylan's prose-poetry. Given the working title of *Side One* and scheduled for a 1966 publication date, the project was delayed because of Dylan's motorcycle accident in July 1966 and not released until 1971 as the experimental novel *Tarantula*, for which Dylan was touted as "a young James Joyce."[84]

BY THE WAY #5

Dylan's References to New York

New York appears intermittently throughout Dylan's more than six-hundred-song oeuvre. The following songs specifically mention places in New York or famous New Yorkers, such as mobster Joey Gallo and comedian Lenny Bruce:

- "NYC Blues" (draft version)
- "Talking New York"
- "Hard Times in New York Town"
- "Talkin' Folklore Center" (a poem that Dylan wrote as a homage to Center founder Izzy Young and that was subsequently published as a broadsheet by the center)
- "Talkin' World War III Blues"
- "Spanish Harlem Incident"
- "I Shall Be Free No. 10"
- "Just Like Tom Thumb's Blues"
- "Positively 4th Street"
- "Dirge"
- "Joey"
- "Sara"
- "Visions of Johanna"
- "Lenny Bruce"

"I DO BELIEVE I'VE HAD ENOUGH"

Dylan was spending less time in the city and more time in Upstate New York, where his manager, Albert Grossman, had a house. In July 1965, Dylan and Sara moved into their own space, an eleven-room Arts and Crafts mansion on Camelot Road named Hi Lo Ha in the tiny hamlet and former artist's colony of Byrdcliffe, less than two miles from the center of Woodstock. Dylan bought it for a pittance—only $12,000. He would later move to a house on the more secluded Ohayo Mountain Road.

Byrdcliffe was founded in 1902 by a wealthy English entrepreneur named Ralph Radcliffe Whitehead, an admirer of John Ruskin and

William Morris and the entire Arts and Crafts movement. Intended to be a home for independent artists, the Byrdcliffe School of Art was the first permanent art school in New York's Hudson Valley. At various times, resident artists of the colony included Aaron Copland and John Cage.

On the morning of July 29, 1966, Dylan crashed his red Triumph 350 motorcycle near Hi Lo Ha, breaking several vertebrae in his neck. (He had bought the bike from photographer Barry Feinstein, who was Mary Travers's husband at the time.) Much mystery surrounded the incident. There were rumors that he had died or was seriously injured. Dylan took advantage of the confusion: he withdrew from the public eye, recovering from the physical wounds and reassessing his career in private.

The oracle of a generation was weary from the constant demands placed on him. He didn't tour again for eight years.

6

MADNESS, MADNESS EVERYWHERE

*D*ylan spent the rest of 1966 recuperating at his Woodstock home. By February 1967, he was hard at work on a mysterious project consisting primarily of down-to-earth songs and ballads: rural music that was remarkably similar to Harry Smith's *Anthology of American Folk Music* that he had listened to back in Dinkytown and in the Village. He was, he said, "making music and watching time go by." He invited a few friends up, members of the backup band he used on the road called the Hawks but better known today as The Band. Rick Danko, Richard Manuel and Garth Hudson came, joined later by Robbie Robertson. For $275 a month, Danko, Manuel and Hudson rented a large pink house in the village of West Saugerties that they soon named Big Pink. Every day, Dylan drove over to Big Pink to hang out.[85] (According to Barney Hoskyns, the rent was considerably lower: $125 a month.) As of 2020, the famous house is available for holiday rental (although, significantly, not the basement) for $550 per night with a two-night minimum.

During the summer of 1967, the band recorded songs in a series of loose and casual sessions in the basement of Big Pink. Although the songs were original, they had deep roots in the American South and, going further back, in Scotland and England. Bootleg versions turned up over and over again, while such artists as Peter, Paul and Mary, the Byrds and Manfred Mann covered much of Dylan's original material and, in the case of Manfred Mann's "The Mighty Quinn," took it to the top of the charts.

Big Pink

Bob Dylan assumed the role of the reclusive hermit, playing and creating music and reading the Bible and the works of William Blake, far removed from the troubles of the world. Ever the contrarian, he continued to do the opposite of what was expected of him. He had had it "with the whole scene." Instead, he savored the timelessness of the countryside to work on a project that tried to recapture a lost, bucolic past. He eschewed a fancy, modern studio in favor of the basement of the rambling Big Pink. Like the *Basement Tapes*, which were recorded in 1967 but not released until 1975, the acoustic-based *John Wesley Harding*, released in January 1968, recalls an older America, consisting of country- and folk-tinged songs rich in biblical overtones. As the rest of the country was getting turned on, Dylan was returning to the basics.[86]

The same month that *John Wesley Harding* was released, Dylan returned to New York, ready to face the public again. He performed at the Woody Guthrie Memorial Concert at Carnegie Hall. (Guthrie had passed away three months earlier.) Backed by the Crackers (another pseudonym for The Band), Dylan appeared at two concerts: one in the afternoon, one in the evening. Other performers included Pete Seeger, Judy Collins, Arlo Guthrie, Richie Havens, Odetta and Tom Paxton. Around the same time, Dylan was asked to play Woody Guthrie in a film project that never came to fruition. He was considered again for the role in 1975 and even went as far as to discuss it with Guthrie's manager, Harold Leventhal. Ultimately, the part went to David Carradine. *Bound for Glory*, its eventual title, was released in 1976.

On and Off Broadway

Shortly after attending his father's funeral in Minnesota in June 1968 and returning home to Woodstock, Dylan received a letter from the poet Archibald MacLeish. MacLeish wanted Dylan to compose songs for a play he was writing called *Scratch*, based on Stephen Vincent Benét's short story "The Devil and Daniel Webster." MacLeish, who considered Dylan a serious poet, appreciated his songs and thought he would be the perfect writing partner. Dylan wasn't convinced, although he had toyed with the idea of writing a play.

Dylan visited MacLeish at the poet's home outside Conway, Massachusetts, and considered MacLeish's suggestions for some possible song titles. But the

BY THE WAY #6

North Country Blues

The wistful "Girl from the North Country" from *The Freewheelin'
Bob Dylan* (1963) takes its inspiration, and its melody, from
the traditional English Child ballad "Scarborough Fair,"
which in turn bears some resemblance to the traditional Scots
Child ballad "The Elfin Knight"—both involve performing
impossible tasks to prove one's love. The song's most famous
version is arguably Simon and Garfunkel's 1965 hit, but Dylan
first learned it from the English singer Martin Carthy while
in England and borrowed his arrangement. Both songs have
a yearning and haunting quality. In "Scarborough Fair," the
narrator laments that his sweetheart "was once a true love of
mine." Dylan uses the same line, with a very slight variation, in
his song, prefaced by "Remember me to one who lives there."
But he also adds various wintry North Country details: the
howling winds, falling snowflakes and frozen rivers.

Irish playwright Conor McPherson captured the elegiac mood
of the song in his *Girl from the North Country*, which he adapted and
directed and which opened on March 5, 2020, at the Belasco
Theater on Broadway before the coronavirus epidemic led to a
sudden shutdown. (It was previously staged at London's Old Vic
in 2017 and at New York's Public Theater in 2018. It reopened
on Broadway in October 2021.)

Set in a boardinghouse in Duluth, Minnesota—Dylan's
birthplace—in 1934 during the Great Depression, the Broadway
musical is built around Dylan's songs and the drifters, lonesome
hobos and wayfaring strangers that inhabit them. It may be a
musical, but it is far from a jukebox musical; it has more in
common with, say, Sherwood Anderson's bleak short-story
collection *Winesburg, Ohio* than *Jersey Boys*. The more than twenty
selections are a combination of well-known songs ("Slow Train,"
"I Want You," "Like a Rolling Stone," "Jokerman," "Sweetheart
Like You," "Hurricane," "All Along the Watchtower," "Forever
Young" and the title track) and obscure ones ("Sign on the
Window," "True Love Tends to Forget," "Duquesne Whistle,"

"Señor (Tales of Yankee Power)," "Is Your Love in Vain?"). The albums represented span the decades, from the 1960s to 2012: *The Freewheelin' Bob Dylan, John Wesley Harding, Highway 61 Revisited, Blonde on Blonde, New Morning, Planet Waves, The Basement Tapes, Blood on the Tracks, Desire, Saved, Infidels, Street-Legal, Empire Burlesque, Time Out of Mind* and *Tempest*.

There is no direct discernible connection between Dylan's lyrics and the action onstage. Instead, the emotions the cast expresses come through in the songs that they sing and in the way they sing them. The music doesn't tell the story; the songs *support* the story. McPherson's version evokes, in tone and mood, Dylan's own collection of North Country songs—not only the eponymous title song but also such plainspoken ballads as "North Country Blues" and "Ballad of Hollis Brown," as well as the Dylan of the Dinkytown and Gaslight eras and the

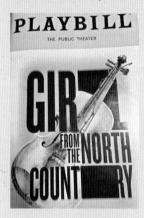

Girl from the North Country playbill. Conor McPherson's musical based on Dylan's wistful song made its North American premiere at New York's Public Theater on October 1, 2018. It made its Broadway premiere at the Belasco Theatre on March 5, 2020, until the pandemic shut it down. It reopened on Broadway in October 2021. *Author collection.*

closing of the mines, the destruction of farms and an overall feeling of displacement and apprehension. Its themes reflect Dylan's songs—social justice, inequality, love and loss, salvation and redemption—with lyrics that recall its midwestern setting, such as when the narrator of "Went to See the Gypsy" watches the sunrise "from that little Minnesota town." It embodies the working-class blues of the people who Dylan knew or read about on the Mesabi Iron Range. It ends on a transcendent note with the sublime "Forever Young."

For some of the younger cast members, working on *Girl from the North Country* was the first time they had heard a Dylan song. Others first heard Dylan on television shows (*Mad Men*) or through other artists (Adele's version of "Make You Feel My Love" or gospel singer Shirley Caesar's "Gotta

Serve Somebody"). Still others had no idea that Dylan had written "Blowin' in the Wind." At least one cast member, the twentysomething Jeannette Bayardelle, whose parents are from Haiti, wasn't familiar with his music at all and yet felt that the songs were "tugging on my soul," she told the *New York Times*'s Elizabeth Vincentelli. "It was familiar yet very spiritual." Todd Almond, another cast member, referred to Dylan's "secret language" and how much his songs have penetrated pop culture. "You don't even know how much you know this material."

Dylan was able to see the show before the pandemic forced it to close and told historian Douglas Brinkley that when the curtain came down, he was "stunned." "I saw it as an anonymous spectator….The play had me crying at the end. I can't even say why."

more Dylan talked to MacLeish about the play, the more he realized that he was not the person for the job. "After hearing a few lines from the script, I didn't see how our destinies could be intermixed," he recalls in *Chronicles*. Still, out of respect, he told MacLeish he would think it over.[87]

Three songs Dylan wrote for the play, "Father of Night," "Time Passes Slowly" and "New Morning," were on his 1970 album *New Morning*. (The songs never did appear in the play; instead, MacLeish used older songs from the Dylan canon.)

Scratch opened on Broadway at the St. James Theater on May 6, 1971, starring Patrick Magee as Daniel Webster and Will Geer as Scratch. It closed two days later.

Decades later, Dylan's songs returned to Broadway for another abbreviated run. In 2006, Dylan collaborated with choreographer Twyla Tharp on the musical *The Times They Are A-Changin'*. Tharp had envisioned a coming-of-age story set in a traveling circus dream world. It premiered on Broadway at the **Brooks Atkinson Theater (42)**, 256 West Forty-Seventh Street, on October 26, 2006, and closed shortly thereafter following disastrous reviews. Critic Terry Teachout, for one, thought the production was so bad that "it makes you forget how good the songs are."[88] In *The Collaborative Habit*, Tharp says that the show was financially draining and physically exhausting. Her biggest mistake, she admits, was to veer away from her original idea: to create a show based on the singer's love songs. "To have used them," she writes, "and dramatized the relationships they suggest might have produced a show I could feel more intensely."[89]

The ill-fated *The Times They Are A-Changin'* was the last time a Dylan-themed musical appeared on Broadway until 2020, when Conor Mcpherson's critically acclaimed *Girl from the North Country* had its premiere on the Great White Way.

WOODSTOCK NATION

In the spring of 1969, Dylan and his family—by this time he had three children, and son Jakob was on the way—moved from Byrdcliffe to a farm in a more remote area of Woodstock on Ohayo Mountain. Although Dylan had originally moved to Woodstock to get away from the craziness of the city, the madness followed him. Unwelcome guests and intruders tried to break into his house day and night, turning what he had hoped would be a quiet refuge from urban chaos into a nightmarish hell. While the world was waiting eagerly for his next masterpiece and his return as a rock 'n' roll superstar, Dylan was fantasizing about living a mundane nine-to-five existence. "Everything was wrong, the world was absurd. It was backing me into a corner."[90]

A group of entrepreneurs decided to organize a music festival to capitalize on the popularity of the Monterey Pop Festival. They chose Woodstock, because it was easily accessible from New York City, it had a reputation as an artists' colony and, more important, the spokesman of youth culture lived there. But reports of drug abuse and violence at other festivals alarmed the locals, who forced the festival setting to move to the dairy farm of forty-nine-year-old Max Yasgur near the town of Bethel, New York, more than forty miles away. Still, the name stuck. Woodstock it would be.

EVERYONE EXPECTED DYLAN TO be there. But Dylan wanted nothing to do with the festival or the so-called Woodstock Nation. "We couldn't *breathe*," Dylan told *Rolling Stone*'s Kurt Loder in 1984. "I couldn't get any space for myself and my family, and there was no help, nowhere. I got very resentful about the whole thing, and we got outta there." While hundreds of thousands of people trudged to Yasgur's farm and wallowed in the sun, rain and mud, Dylan took off to perform at another festival, on the Isle of Wight, off the southern coast of England. (Dylan did perform at Woodstock, twenty-five

BY THE WAY #7

By the Time I Got to Woodstock

Many musicians are associated with the town of Woodstock. In addition to Dylan and members of The Band, they include Van Morrison, Jimi Hendrix, Tim Hardin, Todd Rundgren and Maria Muldaur, to name just a few. They performed at such places as the Café Espresso, the Sled Hill Café, the Elephant, the Village Jug, the Watering Troff, the Squash Blossom, Rosa's Cantina, the Bear Café and the Little Bear. (Ironically, the most famous song about Woodstock, the Joni Mitchell classic, was written by someone—Mitchell—who never lived in the town.)

Dylan's favorite coffeehouse in town was the Café Espresso on Tinker Street. It had a classic decor and atmosphere: red-and-white check tablecloth and a jukebox that played classical music. Live music was also presented on weekend nights and Sunday afternoons. Performers included Dave Van Ronk, Tom Paxton, Patrick Sky, Phil Ochs, Jack Elliott, Joan Baez, John Hammond Jr., the Reverend Gary Davis and Mississippi John Hurt. For all intents and purposes, Café Espresso was the rural outpost of a Village coffeehouse.

Dylan didn't perform at the Espresso, though. He hung out there, safe in the realization that no one would bother him. It was a place where he could relax and be himself. He drank coffee, played chess, read the *New York Times*, smoked cigarettes and wrote. The owners, Bernard and Mary Lou Paturel, allowed him to work in an upstairs room. The so-called White Room had windows overlooking Tinker Street as well as a couch and a desk. Sometimes, he would even stay overnight. It was here, according to Barney Hoskyns, author of *Small Town Talk*, where he wrote, "It Ain't Me, Babe" and "My Back Pages."

The Café Espresso space is now the Center for Photography at Woodstock.

In addition to Dylan's *The Basement Tapes*, other famous recordings associated with the town include The Band's *Music from Big Pink*, Van Morrison's *Moondance* and Todd Rundgren's

> *The Hermit of Mink Hollow.* In 2014, the New Basement Tapes, consisting of Jim James, Elvis Costello, Marcus Mumford, Taylor Goldsmith and Rhiannon Giddens, released *Lost on the River*, an album of tracks with songs written by Dylan in 1967 during the recording of the original *Basement Tapes.*

years later. He put in an appearance at the Woodstock '94 festival, held in August in Saugerties, near the original site.)[91]

When Dylan returned from England, the craziness continued. Upstate New York became too much to bear. Recalling good memories, Dylan decided to move his family back to Greenwich Village. To Dylan, the move made sense in a counterintuitive way. He liked the Village, he knew the Village, he felt safe in the Village. In another era—only a few years before—the Village had functioned as his urban cocoon. Village residents respected his privacy. The Village would offer protection. When, in late 1969, he learned that a handsome nineteenth-century townhouse at **94 MacDougal Street (43)** was available, he bought it "sight unseen." Located across the street from Caffe Dante, it was just a few blocks away from his old haunts.

But the Village that Dylan returned to was not the same place he had left in the mid-1960s. Everything had changed. Demonstrators found his house "and paraded up and down in front of it chanting and shouting, demanding for me to come out and lead them somewhere, he recalled, and to "stop shirking my duties as the conscience of a generation." This did not endear him to the neighbors. Worse, Dylan was constantly harassed by A.J. Weberman, the infamous "Dylanologist" who rummaged through the musician's garbage as if searching for buried treasure, looking for clues to some great mystery.[92]

Dylan told an interviewer that "the stimulation had vanished. Everybody was in a pretty down mood. It was over."[93] In retrospect, Dylan admitted that returning to the Village was "a stupid thing to do." Woodstock Nation had taken over MacDougal Street, too.[94]

One of the few places where he could escape the chaos was a rented colonial house in East Hampton on Long Island—he used his mother's maiden name to avoid publicity—that had belonged to Henry Ford and was located "on a quiet street with majestic old elms." The house had an expansive backyard and a key to a "gated dune" that led to a sandy beach.

Dylan's salmon-colored townhouse on MacDougal Street, across from Dante, formerly known as Caffe Dante. *Photo by author.*

Dylan considered himself a family man, and he enjoyed playing the role of father (by this time, he and Sara had five children, including one from Sara's previous marriage): beachcombing with the kids, boating on the bay, digging for clams, visiting lighthouses and hunting for buried treasure.[95]

BLOOD ON THE TRACKS

Dylan had long been interested in painting. Back in his Village days, Suze Rotolo had introduced him to the work of Red Grooms. While in East Hampton, he began to paint landscapes as well as portraits, including his own self-portrait, which appeared on the album of the same name. (Dylan also did the cover painting for The Band's *Music from Big Pink*.)

Self-Portrait was released in June 1970 to mostly bad reviews, although in recent years critics have been willing not only to give it a second chance but also to claim it as an overlooked gem. Even so, this is the record about which critic Greil Marcus famously asked, "What is this shit?" Recorded partly in New York and partly in Nashville, it is an odd album in the Dylan canon, consisting of cover versions and Dylanesque reworkings of standards. His next album, *New Morning*, came out a mere four months later and includes the songs he had written for the aborted Archibald MacLeish musical.[96]

In August 1971, Dylan appeared at the first charity event concert in popular music, the Concert for Bangladesh at **Madison Square Garden (44)**, 4 Penn Plaza. Organized by George Harrison, two charity concerts were held for the relief of refugees in the Asian country of Bangladesh, formerly known as East Pakistan. In addition to Harrison and Dylan, the performers included Eric Clapton, Billy Preston, Leon Russell, Badfinger and Ringo Starr. Harrison introduced Dylan, who took the stage and sang "Love Minus Zero," "Just Like a Woman," "It Takes a Lot to Laugh, It Takes a Train to Cry," "Mr. Tambourine Man," "A Hard Rain's A-Gonna Fall" and "Blowin' in the Wind."

Meanwhile, Dylan took a hiatus from urban life: he went to Mexico to appear in Sam Peckinpah's film *Pat Garrett and Billy the Kid*, in which he played a character named "Alias." The movie costarred James Coburn as Pat Garrett and Kris Kristofferson as Billy the Kid. Dylan wrote and sang the title song, "Knockin' on Heaven's Door," as well as the score for the entire soundtrack; both the movie and the soundtrack were released in 1973.

Dylan continued writing new songs, which would evolve into the introspective and nostalgic *Planet Waves*. Released in early 1974, the album is significant for several reasons: it boasts one of his best and most enduringly popular and versatile songs, "Forever Young," and it features on the back cover one of Dylan's fictional autobiographical prose-poems. "The old days are gone forever," he writes, "and the new ones ain't far behind."

In January 1974, Dylan embarked on a forty-date, six-week North American tour with members of The Band, including three shows at Madison Square Garden. It was the first time in eight years that Dylan had toured. Demand for tickets was strong—not surprising, since he had been away for such a long time. Dylan biographer Howard Sounes goes so far as to call the tour "the first major stadium tour of the rock era." The tour resulted in a double live album, *Before the Flood*, released in June 1974. The album was a huge popular and critical success, reaching number three on the *Billboard* charts and considered by some critics as one of the best live albums of its day.[97]

After the tour ended, Dylan had to face reality. His marriage to Sara was failing. Part of their problem may seem insignificant—bickering over details of a mansion Dylan was remodeling near Malibu, California—but the seemingly trivial issues were indicative of larger problems, which included Dylan's wandering eye. They eventually divorced in 1977.

Dylan felt the urge to return to painting, but at a more serious and sophisticated level. Painting was not only therapeutic but also helped unleash different aspects of his creativity. In the spring of 1974, he attended group-painting classes by the seventy-three-year-old artist Norman Raeben at his eleventh-floor studio in Carnegie Hall. Dylan dropped in one day and stayed two months. He was a dedicated and serious student, attending all-day classes five days a week. The classes were intense. "That's all I did for two months," he explains. His fellow students were a broad cross section of people from all walks of life, including wealthy elderly ladies, an off-duty police officer, a bus driver and a lawyer. Significantly, Raeben didn't know who Dylan was. He thought he was some scruffy lost soul who had somehow wandered into his class.[98]

The Russian-born Raeben had studied with George Luks, Robert Henri and John Sloan—all members of the Ashcan School, a realist style of American painting. Raeben's father was the Yiddish writer Sholom Aleichem, who created the character of Tevye, the protagonist in the musical *Fiddler on the Roof*. Raeben and his techniques made a profound impact on Dylan's next album, *Blood on the Tracks*, which chronicles the deterioration of a relationship, namely, his faltering relationship with Sara.

Raeben taught Dylan how to see in an entirely new way—to look at an object, look away and then draw it—and to do consciously what he unconsciously felt. *Blood on the Tracks* was the first album Dylan made using this new perspective. Raeben also gave Dylan a new perspective on writing and helped him reconsider the concept of time. Dispensing with linear usage, Dylan wrote lyrics that played with time that combined past, present and future while offering various narrative perspectives. The songs on *Blood on the Tracks* float in a place, says Dylan, where "there is no time." He tried "to make the focus as strong as a magnifying glass....To do that consciously is a trick," he explained, "and I did it on *Blood on the Tracks* for the first time."[99]

Meanwhile, Dylan spent the summer of 1974 on a farm in Minnesota that he had bought with his younger brother, David. He started to write a series of songs that he referred to as "private songs," that is, songs not initially intended for public consumption. In mid-September, he booked studio time at A&R Studios at 799 Seventh Avenue—previously known as Columbia's Studio A—and laid down an album's worth of material. But Dylan had doubts about the songs. He felt a vague dissatisfaction with them and was unhappy with at least half of the tracks. Around Christmas 1974, even as Columbia was preparing for a pending release, Dylan's brother suggested that they go into a local studio to rerecord the album. Dylan agreed and decided to start all over again, replacing half the songs that he had already recorded, but this time with a pickup band that he didn't know in a Minneapolis record studio, during the waning days of 1974.

When *Blood on the Tracks* was released in early 1975, it was hailed as a masterpiece. To this day, it remains among Dylan's most acclaimed albums. It contains some of his most enduring songs, such as "Tangled Up in Blue," "Simple Twist of Fate," "Shelter from the Storm" and the ballad "Lily, Rosemary, and the Jack of Hearts."

7

SOMETHING LIKE A CIRCUS

By the summer of 1975, Dylan was revitalized. His tour with The Band the previous year had been a success, even though it left him spent and exhausted. He was without a manager—he had terminated his contract with Albert Grossman in July 1970 after years of a strained relationship. Grossman did not agree with Dylan's decision to stop touring after the singer's devastating accident in 1966. But more than this, they just saw things differently. Conditions didn't come to a head until 1981, when Grossman filed a lawsuit against Dylan claiming that the singer owed him tens of thousands of dollars in back royalties. Dylan, in turn, countersued, alleging that Grossman had mismanaged his career. The suit wasn't settled until 1987, by which point Grossman was dead.

Thus, by 1975, Dylan was completely on his own again, both professionally and personally, and ready to start over. In June, he was living by himself in the Village, visiting his old haunts, checking out new ones and socializing with friends along MacDougal, Bleecker, and Third Streets at places like Gerde's, the Kettle of Fish, the Dug Out and the Other End.

It didn't take long for word to spread that Dylan was making the rounds of the clubs again. His presence in the Village did not go unnoticed by the press, either. In late June, he made a surprise appearance at the **Bottom Line (45)**, 15 West Fourth Street (now closed). He spent so much time hanging out in the Village (many of the musicians on *Desire*, which he was working on, came from there) that the *Village Voice* asked, "Will MacDougal St. Rise Again?"

In a brilliant marketing move, Paul Colby, owner of the **Other End** and the **Bitter End (46)**, started the First Annual Village Folk Festival. Colby knew full well that it wasn't the first such festival, but he couldn't resist a little exaggeration. As he noted, "hyperbole was always standard advertising procedure in the Village." Dylan made an appearance at the festival. He hung out with such old friends as Ramblin' Jack Elliott and Bobby Neuwirth at the Other End. For a time, Dylan made almost nightly appearances at the Bitter End, located next door at 147 Bleecker Street. Colby connected the two clubs. "I was able to run a separate restaurant and even keep a pool table," he said. (On July 23, 1992, the City of New York granted landmark status to the club.)[100]

Colby reserved a booth for Dylan so Dylan could retain an element of privacy. "I made sure no one bothered him," he said. To Dylan, it was a laid-back version of the old days. "He was so happy and relaxed." Sometimes Dylan was content to sit in the audience or play pool, but he also often took to the stage. Others dropped by, too. Some were old friends (Dave Van Ronk, Phil Ochs); others were musicians brought in by Neuwirth, including Loudon Wainwright III, Mick Ronson and T-Bone Burnett. During the Fourth of July weekend, Dylan joined Ramblin' Jack Elliott on stage at the Other End, played guitar with Elliott on Woody Guthrie's "Pretty Boy Floyd" and even debuted a new song, "Abandoned Love."[101]

Dylan was a musical catalyst. Because of his reappearance on the scene, a new generation of fresh faces was drawn to the Village, including Tom Verlaine, Steve Forbert, Willy Nile and Patti Smith. Of this new generation, Smith was a revelation to Dylan. He saw her perform at the Other End on June 26. Like him, she was influenced by Rimbaud and the Beats, and she combined hard-edged rock with a poet's sensibility. A Jersey girl born in Chicago, she had arrived in New York in 1967, just a half dozen years after Dylan, but Dylan was one of her cultural heroes. Sharing a second-floor apartment at 160 Hall Street in Brooklyn with photographer Robert Mapplethorpe for eighty dollars a month—she later moved to 45 MacDougal Street—Smith hung photographs of Dylan along with Rimbaud, Piaf and Lennon over her desk, staying up late reading comic books and listening to the transplanted Minnesotan.

In July 1975, Dylan ran into Jacques Levy, a songwriter, theater director, professor and psychologist who cowrote songs with Roger McGuinn of the Byrds and had roots in Brechtian and experimental theater. They had met each other on and off over the years. Dylan was aware of Levy mostly through his work with McGuinn and the Byrds—in 1969, Levy cowrote "Chestnut

The Bitter End. In 1961, Fred Weintraub opened the former coffeehouse-turned-nightclub. For a few years, it was known as the Other End before returning to its original name. During the early '60s, the club presented hootenannies on Tuesday nights. It was granted landmark status in 1992. *Photo by author.*

Mare" with McGuinn as part of a country-rock theatrical adaptation of Ibsen's *Peer Gynt* to be called *Gene Tryp*. It never was staged, although the song became one of the Byrds' bigger hits.

One day in July, Levy walked out of his LaGuardia Place loft while Dylan was walking around the corner on Bleecker Street en route to the Other End. (They had met the same way the previous summer.) This time, the two men began to chat; Dylan ended up coming up to Levy's apartment. Dylan suggested that they write something together, a major departure from his usual working methods and seemingly out of character (although Dylan would later collaborate with other writers, from Sam Shepard to Grateful Dead lyricist Robert Hunter). But Dylan was in an expansive mood, open to new ideas and new ways of working, and the unexpected connection with Levy would change his approach to writing songs.

Dylan played "bits and pieces of some songs" for Levy on the piano. They began collaborating that evening, working through the night; by dawn, they had come up with their first project, the autobiographical "Isis," an enigmatic song about a man who is separated from his spouse and the adventures he experiences on the road. They continued their collaboration, experimenting at Dylan's beach house on Long Island and trying out new material in Village clubs, in two weeks writing most of the material that would appear on *Desire*. In total, Dylan and Levy worked together on seven songs on the album. Only two songs, "Sara" and "One More Cup of Coffee," were penned by Dylan alone.

Brother Bob's All-Star Traveling Minstrel Show

For years, Dylan had dreamed of putting together a touring revue that would consist of a core group of musicians—a traveling caravan of musicians—along with guest artists. The time he spent that summer and early fall in the Village clubs convinced Dylan that such a production could be done.

In the back room of the Other End, Dylan asked Ramblin' Jack Elliott if he would like to join him as part of "a little tour" that would play gigs around New England with Neuwirth and Baez. The idea behind the tour was to perform in small towns and small halls like a traveling minstrel-carnival-medicine-vaudeville show that, in its loosely conceived format, recalled Dylan's own fantasy vagabond life out West. In a way, it was a precursor of sorts of his modern Never Ending Tour.

As the months progressed, Dylan asked more and more artists to join. Joan Baez said yes, as did an unknown Texan guitarist by the name of Henry "T-Bone" Burnett. Eventually, Dylan's gypsy band of performers would include Neuwirth, McGuinn, Baez, Elliott, Ronson, Scarlet Rivera, Ronee Blakley, Ronnie Hawkins and Arlo Guthrie. Allen Ginsberg was asked to recite poetry—he and fellow poet Anne Waldman were given the official titles of "poets in residence"—while Jacques Levy was hired as the stage manager.

Dylan, an erstwhile cinema buff, decided to make a movie of the tour and hired a young, aspiring playwright named Sam Shepard to write the script. Dylan asked Shepard if he had ever seen the François Truffaut movie *Shoot the Piano Player*—one of Dylan's favorite films. "Is that the kind of movie you want to make?" asked Shepard. "Something like that," Dylan replied. Shepard never did write that script, but he did publish the *Rolling Thunder Logbook*, an impressionistic diary of the tour.[102]

Dylan went back to New York at the end of the summer and then spent some time in Minneapolis before returning to the city in mid-October to make the final preparations for the show. While the revue musicians were in rehearsals, he stayed at the **Gramercy Park Hotel (47)** at 2 Lexington Avenue. For many years a run-down hotel with character, it is now a luxury boutique hotel. During the 1970s, it was a favorite of visiting rock musicians, from the Clash to David Bowie.

On October 23, 1975, Dylan and various members of the Rolling Thunder Revue, as it was now called—in a very fluid and ever-changing lineup—went down to Gerde's Folk City to celebrate owner Mike Porco's sixty-first birthday. The evening was an informal, and shambling, dress rehearsal for the revue—and it was all captured on camera as part of Dylan's film *Renaldo and Clara*. It was a topsy-turvy night: Joan Baez joined Dylan on stage on "One Too Many Mornings"—the first time they had performed together in ten years. Neuwirth recited a poem; Ginsberg sang a song. Phil Ochs, eager to please ("I want to do my best, I want to do it for everybody and I want to do it for Bob"), took the stage and sang five songs. Bette Midler, before she became known as the "Divine Miss M," performed. Patti Smith, dressed in black, quickly got on and off the stage.[103]

The Rolling Thunder Revue officially opened on October 30, 1975, at the War Memorial Auditorium in Plymouth, Massachusetts. In December, Dylan returned to Madison Square Garden as part of the Revue for a benefit concert called "The Night of the Hurricane," in support of Rubin "Hurricane" Carter, the middleweight boxer who many, including Dylan, believed was falsely accused of murder. (Dylan and Jacques Levy cowrote a protest song about Carter, "Hurricane," that appears on *Desire*. More than eight minutes long, it provoked a storm of controversy when it was released, because Dylan played fast and loose with the facts.) The Rolling Thunder Revue tour ended on May 25, 1976, at the most unlikely of places: the Salt Palace in Salt Lake City, before a half-full auditorium.

Dylan's four-hour-long *Renaldo and Clara*, released in 1978, chronicles aspects of the revue, combining concert footage, rambling interviews, amateurishly staged segments and other surrealistic, Fellini-esque bits and pieces. Considered by some a "radical masterpiece" and dismissed by others as a boring, pretentious, egocentric exercise in self-indulgence, it is nevertheless a fascinating, if messy, document of a time and place.

In 2019, Martin Scorsese released *Rolling Thunder Revue: A Bob Dylan Story*, which covers the Rolling Thunder concert tour but largely consists of outtakes from Dylan's *Renaldo and Clara*.

Dylan's mid-1970s sojourn in the Village was but a temporary respite from the demons that were haunting him; by the end of the decade, he was at a crossroads. Although he continued to visit New York, he was spending much of his time on the West Coast. He was also dealing with a very public and messy divorce, custody battles and alimony payments—big ones.

In many ways, the late 1970s were lost years for Dylan. After the critical and popular success of *Blood on the Tracks* in 1975 and the release of *Desire* the following year, Dylan spent virtually all of 1977 working on *Renaldo and Clara*. He also took time to record *Street-Legal* in Santa Monica, California, using a rehearsal space that he, perhaps prophetically, called Rundown Studios. The album contains some fine songs, but with his divorce to Sara about to be finalized, Dylan was at wit's end. His personal life had turned into a chaotic mess, and his professional life was about to enter the nadir of his career.

While Dylan's life was in turmoil, so were the fortunes of New York City. President Gerald Ford's refusal in 1975 to provide emergency federal aid to rescue the faltering city from near-certain economic collapse led the *New York Daily News* to print the now-famous headline "Ford to City, Drop Dead!" The blackout of 1977, which led to widespread looting and vandalism, and the murder spree by serial killer David "Son of Sam" Berkowitz, who terrorized New York from July 1976 to his arrest in August 1977 (and was dramatized by Spike Lee in his 1999 film *Summer of Sam*), were emblematic of the chaos at the time.

Things would get worse before they got better for New York. From the mid-1980s to the early 1990s, crime rose sharply, fueled by a virulent crack cocaine epidemic. Residents lived in fear behind doors with multiple locks. Several days before Christmas 1984, the so-called subway vigilante, Bernard Goetz, shot four young men on a Manhattan subway who were trying to rob him. Conditions were so bad that in 1990, *Time* magazine published a cover story insisting that the Big Apple should more properly be called the Rotting Apple. But the warning signs had been present as early as the late 1960s. Saul Bellow captures the darkened mood in his 1970 novel *Mr. Sammler's Planet*, a cautionary tale in which a Holocaust survivor must find a way to survive in a city where civilization is unraveling at the seams. The streets were full of hoodlums, and the city's coffers were empty.

Yet, economic decline had its advantages. A fall in the overall standard of living in the 1970s led to lower rents and to the growth, in at least one neighborhood, of a thriving alternative culture: the American punk movement, which made its unofficial headquarters in the gritty East Village. Meanwhile, in the Bronx, the first rumblings of a strange and exciting new music were being heard: hip-hop.

Born Again

Near the end of a world tour in late 1978, Dylan claimed that Jesus visited him in an Arizona hotel room. "Jesus put his hand on me," he said. "It was a physical thing. I felt it. I felt it all over me. I felt my whole body tremble. The glory of the Lord knocked me down and picked me up." In early 1979, he started attending Bible school in Los Angeles. "I had always read the Bible, but I only looked at it as literature. I was never really instructed in it in a way that was meaningful to me." He was introduced to pastors from the Vineyard Fellowship in West Los Angeles and began an intensive course on Bible study in the mornings.[104]

Dylan fully accepted Jesus Christ as his lord and savior. In was during this "born again" period that he released several Christian-themed albums. *Slow Train Coming* in 1979 confirmed Dylan's conversion to Christianity. Many of his fans hated it—perhaps still do. It was followed by *Saved* in 1980 and *Shot of Love* in 1981. Both were commercial disappointments.

Nomadland

Although Dylan was moving farther and farther away from New York, both geographically and in spirit, he didn't abandon the city entirely. He returned throughout the years to record albums such as *Infidels* in 1983 and parts of *Empire Burlesque* in 1985 at the **Power Station (48)**, at 441 West Fifty-Third Street, which was housed in an old Consolidated Edison building. Dylan recorded what many critics consider to be among his finest songs, "Blind Willie McTell," during these sessions. Ostensibly, it is a nearly six-minute song about the great prewar blues musician Blind Willie McTell (1898–1959), but it is so much more than that: it is, in effect, the story of America's original sin, slavery, as seen through the lens of a blues song. (Dylan scholar Michael Gray devoted a chapter to the song in his book *Song & Dance Man III: The Art of Bob Dylan*. He also wrote about McTell in *Hand Me My Travelin' Shoes: In Search of Blind Willie McTell*.)

Infidels was hailed as Dylan's comeback album and a return to form, or at least a return to secular music (even though the album does contain songs with religious overtones). His fans rewarded him with enough sales to turn it into a gold record: it even contained a bona fide hit ("Jokerman"), as well as several solid songs and some excellent guitar work from Dire Straits frontman Mark Knopfler, who also produced the album.

Dylan also either rented or owned various buildings throughout Manhattan, including an early twentieth-century four-story, brick townhouse on historic Striver's Row in Harlem at 265 West 139th Street, which he owned from the 1980s until 2000, although he didn't seem to actually live there. (Reports indicate he intended to rent it or lend it to friends.) In 2017, it was on the market for the pre-pandemic price of $3,689,000. In the early 1970s, after leaving Woodstock, he briefly rented a brownstone in the Turtle Bay neighborhood at 242 East 49th Street. His next-door neighbor at the time was none other than Katharine Hepburn; she had lived there for decades. Dylan invited the legendary actress to his daughter's graduation party with a handwritten note. "It will be from 7:30 to 10—if you could stop by, you'd be most welcome," he cheerfully offered. The apartment, he noted in parenthesis, is "the one with the dog." He owned a bullmastiff named Brutus at the time.

Apparently, Hepburn did not attend the party.

But for the most part, Dylan had been a recording nomad since the mid-1980s, laying down tracks in a dizzying number of locations, from New Orleans to Chicago to Florida to his home studio in California.

He occasionally performed at venues around New York, sometimes at unexpected places. In November 1985, Columbia hosted a party—in his honor—at the **Whitney Museum (49)** at 945 Madison Avenue on the Upper East Side to celebrate the release of *Biograph*, the five-LP boxed set that spanned his entire career up to that point. Columbia went all out to promote the recording; the party attracted musicians (Lou Reed, Roger McGuinn, Rick Danko, David Bowie), filmmakers (Martin Scorsese, Paul Schrader) and some old friends from the early Village days, including Harold Leventhal.

In March 1987, he appeared in a tuxedo at a George Gershwin tribute concert at the Brooklyn Academy of Music, performing a solo acoustic version of George and Ira Gershwin's 1927 song "Soon." (In 2015, he released *Shadows in the Night*, his interpretations of pop standards from "Autumn Leaves" to "Some Enchanted Evening.")

On January 20, 1988, Dylan was inducted into the Rock and Roll Hall of Fame in a ceremony held at the **Waldorf-Astoria (50)** at 301 Park Avenue. Some 1,200 guests were in attendance. Other inductees that evening were the Beatles, the Beach Boys, the Drifters, Berry Gordy Jr., the Supremes, Lead Belly and Woody Guthrie. Bruce Springsteen, wearing a silk suit and countrified bolo tie, introduced Dylan. "When I was a kid, Bob's voice somehow—it thrilled and scared me, it made me feel kind of irresponsibly innocent—it still does."[105]

Dylan thanked Springsteen and the board of directors of the Hall of Fame. He acknowledged Muhammad Ali, who was in the audience, and then added, "I'd like to thank a couple of people who are here tonight, who helped me out a great deal coming up. Little Richard....I don't think I would have even started out without listening to Little Richard. And Alan Lomax....I spent many nights in his apartment house, visiting and meeting with all kinds of folk music people, which I never would have come in contact with. And I want to thank Mike Love for not mentioning me," he added. (Love had lashed out at Diana Ross and Paul McCartney for not attending.) "I play a lot of dates every year, too, and peace, love, and harmony is greatly important indeed but so is forgiveness, and we gotta have that too. So thanks."[106]

On October 16, 1992, he returned to Madison Square Garden when Columbia Records hosted a concert to celebrate his career: the three-and-a-half-hour show was broadcast live on pay television. He sang "It's Alright, Ma (I'm Only Bleeding)," "Girl from the North Country" and "My Back Pages," the latter accompanied by Roger McGuinn, Tom Petty, Neil Young, Eric Clapton and George Harrison. Other performers included John Mellencamp, Stevie Wonder, Eddie Vedder, Lou Reed, Tracy Chapman, June Carter and Johnny Cash, Willie Nelson, the Clancy Brothers and Tommy Makem and Rosanne Cash. A six-sided album was released the following year, *Bob Dylan: The 30th Anniversary Concert Celebration*.

In the late 1980s, Dylan began playing smaller venues with a smaller band. This was the beginning of what he called his Never Ending Tour. It is still going strong, or at least a version of it: in September 2021, he announced his Rough and Rowdy Ways Tour 2021–2024. The tour's official poster featured a dapper-dressed, top-hatted skeleton with a syringe in one hand and in another a gift-wrapped box. The hand with the syringe pointed toward the silhouette of a dancing couple. Perhaps it was his way of saying life goes on even in the middle of a pandemic.

Back in November 1993, he performed a remarkable acoustic set with his band at the **Supper Club (51)**, 228 West Forty-Seventh Street, which is now the Hotel Edison. The gig consisted of four acoustic shows over two days; two hundred tickets were distributed free of charge to fans. He had booked the club with the intention of making a concert film for television, but that never came to pass. The show is considered legendary as much for the quality of the performances as for the intimacy of the venue.

Despite his reputation as a visionary modern artist, Dylan always looked to the past. John Hinchey refers to "the history we carry around with us." Dylan carries that history with him every day. From 1989 to 1997, in between touring, he released a series of albums that returned to his Greenwich Village roots. The critically acclaimed *Oh Mercy*, released in 1989, features "Man in the Long Black Coat," which recalls both the traditional Scots ballad "The Daemon Lover," a song that Dylan performed during his early days in the Village, and the 1959 country ballad "The Long Black Veil," about a man falsely accused of murder. *Good as I Been to You*, released in 1992, features such folk and blues classics as "Frankie & Albert," "Blackjack Davey," the Irish song "Arthur McBride" and the seventeenth-century Scottish song "Froggie Went A-Courtin.'" Similarly, *World Gone Wrong*, released the next year, contains the chilling "Love Henry," his rendition of the traditional English folk song "Pretty Polly," the murder ballad "Delia" and a rendition of the African American blues song "Stack a Lee," taken straight from the version by Frank Hutchison that appears on the Harry Smith anthology.[107]

Dylan's resurgence—with the exception of some occasional sparks of brilliance, his career had been in decline for a good part of the 1980s— came to full fruition in September 1997, when he wrote a new set of songs while confined to his Minnesota farm during a particularly snowy winter. The songs on *Time Out of Mind* create a particular mood. "The record is set in another time, the south, Missouri, Mississippi. It's steamboat, civil war, very Mark Twain kinda stuff," said Dylan. *Time Out of Mind* came out a few months after Dylan's near-fatal bout with pericarditis, a severe inflammation around the heart caused by a fungal infection. "I really thought I'd be seeing Elvis soon," he joked in a statement released to the media.[108]

THE SKY SPLIT OPEN

In May 2001, Dylan returned to New York to record *"Love and Theft"* at Sony Music Studios. The album was released on September 11, and in the turmoil surrounding the tragic events of that mournful day, it did not receive the attention it deserved, although it did ultimately reach as high as number five on the *Billboard* charts and garnered uniformly glowing reviews. Today, it is ranked as one of his finest efforts.

Redolent of vintage Americana and steeped in all manner of musical allusions, *"Love and Theft"* evokes the spirit of bluesmen (Robert Johnson, Muddy Waters, Howlin' Wolf, Charley Patton), country icons (Bill Monroe, Dock Boggs), great jazz singers (Billie Holiday) and composers from the so-called Golden Age of American Song (Hoagy Carmichael), as well as references to such literary and historical figures as Lewis Carroll, Charles Darwin and F. Scott Fitzgerald and an oddball assortment of characters.

What makes the album spooky are its seemingly clairvoyant lyrics and its sinister undertones. It's almost as if Dylan knew what was going to happen on that terrible day before anybody else did. "When I left home the sky split open wide," he sings in "Honest with Me," a line that must have hit too close to home that sunny September morning for many New Yorkers.

BY THE WAY #8

Searching for a New Dylan

Imitation, as they say, is the highest form of flattery. After Dylan's first touch of fame in the early 1960s, it didn't take long for mainstream media and record company executives to start their search for the New Dylan. Dylan's former producer John Hammond was constantly pressured by his record company to find "new Dylans." And pronto.

Among the first "new Dylans" were David Blue, Donovan and Patrick Sky. Even Carly Simon, at one point early in her career, was touted as the "female Bob Dylan." The early 1970s saw a few other strong candidates—John Prine, Loudon Wainwright III—but none fit the bill better than Bruce Springsteen. One of the first major pieces written on Springsteen, a profile that appeared in the March 1973 issue of *Crawdaddy*, captured the New Jersey singer at Kenny's Castaways at 157 Bleecker Street in the Village (next door to the Bitter End) and described him as bearing a faint resemblance to Dylan.

There are some striking similarities between Dylan and Springsteen. Like Dylan, Springsteen began his career playing at the Cafe Wha? and the Gaslight. And the two men shared the same producer, John Hammond. For Springsteen, though, being tagged as the New Dylan was a drag ("I don't like it and it's hard to live with").

"Some things are too terrible to be true," he observes. Even more graphic is the ominous "Mississippi," in which the narrator paints a portrait of a sky that is "full of fire / pain pourin' down." The album ends on a note of uncertainty with the dirge-like "Sugar Baby." The singer issues a warning call, "You always got to be prepared but you never know for what," before coming to the chilling conclusion that "happiness can come suddenly and leave just as quick."

Dylan and his Never Ending Tour band played at Madison Square Garden on November 19, a little more than two months after the attacks. "You don't have to ask me how I feel about this town," he told the sold-out crowd. "Most of these songs were written here and the ones that weren't were recorded here." Wearing a pinkish suit and snakeskin cowboy boots and performing before a celebrity-filled audience that included Debra Winger, Chris Rock, Jimmy Fallon and Sheryl Crow, Dylan sang classics ("A Hard Rain's A-Gonna Fall," "Blowin' in the Wind," "Tangled Up in Blue") and new material from *"Love and Theft,"* including "Honest with Me" and "Sugar Baby."[109]

Four years later, in May 2005, Dylan began a series of shows at the **Beacon Theatre (52)**, 2124 Broadway. The Beacon shows coincided with a panel discussion called "His Back Pages: Writers on Dylan" that met at the **Housing Works Bookstore Café (53)**, 126 Crosby Street, in Soho. The panelists discussed Dylan's performances at the Beacon during his five-night run there, which ranged from wonderful to a shambles. They considered the ongoing problem of where to place the piano onstage (in recent years, because Dylan has replaced a guitar with a piano, his back is usually facing the audience). They also wondered why Dylan means so much to them and, by extension, to so many others. David Gates, for example, first saw Dylan at the 1964 Newport Jazz Festival. "I thought he was such a poseur, a fake hillbilly, and I basically couldn't stand him." Jonathan Lethem, on the other hand, considers himself a second-generation Dylanist. He listened to his parents' albums, and the first song he loved as a child was "The Mighty Quinn."[110]

The Beacon was also the site of a tribute concert in 2007 held prior to the release of Todd Haynes's film *I'm Not There*, featuring two dozen songs performed by a wide array of musicians, from Dylan sideman Al Kooper to My Morning Jacket.

8

I AM MANY

Where I'm bound, I can't tell
—Bob Dylan, "Don't Think Twice, It's All Right"

Although there are no official monuments to Bob Dylan in New York, traces of him—some physical, others metaphorical—remain, especially in Greenwich Village. Visitors might experience serendipitous fleeting moments, as I did, when I saw a man passing by wearing a T-shirt with Dylan's face emblazoned on it. On the wall of the music club **Groove (54),** 125 MacDougal Street, is a mural by Rico Fonseca that celebrates the many musicians associated with the Village, including Dylan. (Strumming a guitar with a harmonica holder around his neck, he is next to George Harrison and beneath Joan Baez.) "Keep the spirit of the sixties alive," it says.

Sometimes, coming across an image of Dylan is a matter of timing. I recall walking by Bleecker Bob's Records (118 West Third Street) and seeing a poster advertising *The Times They Are A-Changin'* or another remnant of the old Village, a copy of the album *Bleecker and MacDougal: The Folk Scene of the 1960s*. (As an aside, Bleecker Bob's was a Village institution. In 1967, Robert "Bleecker Bob" Plotnik, a lawyer by trade, collaborated with a record-collector friend, Al Trommers—known as "Broadway Al"—to open the oldies shop, originally located at 149 Bleecker Street before moving to MacDougal Street in the 1970s and finally settling at its Third Street location until it closed in 2013. Plotnik died in November 2018.)

A detail of Dylan with harmonica holder hanging around his neck from a mural at the Groove, a Village nightclub. *Photo by author.*

Dylan's portrait by illustrator Edward Sorel is one among many that graces the wall at the Waverly Inn and Garden (16 Bank Street), a landmark restaurant that opened after World War I and was refurbished in 2006 by *Vanity Fair* editor Graydon Carter. Sorel's Dylan is a curly-headed, frowning fallen angel strumming a lyre with a cigarette hanging from the corner of his mouth. His bohemian companions include Anaïs Nin, Allen Ginsberg, e.e. cummings, Djuna Barnes, Fran Lebowitz, Jackson Pollock, William Burroughs, Eugene O'Neill, Dylan Thomas, Edgar Allan Poe, Norman Mailer, Jack Kerouac, Joan Baez, James Baldwin, Mabel Dodge and John Reed, Jane Jacobs, John Sloan and Andy Warhol. Located below street level, the inn is a series of charming and quaintly cozy rooms with uneven wood floors, low ceilings, fireplaces and red banquettes.

Today, Bob Dylan is as busy as ever. Over the course of his career, he has written more than six hundred songs—and he continues to write new material. He's busy in other ways, too. His memoir *Chronicles*, which he wrote on a manual typewriter in capital letters (according to *Newsweek*'s David Gates, "to make it easier for an assistant to read and retype"), was published in October 2004. In 2011, he signed a six-book deal with publisher Simon & Schuster that includes two additional autobiographical works, although, as of this writing, only *Chronicles* has appeared.[111]

From September 2006 to January 2007, the exhibit "Bob Dylan's American Journey, 1956–1966" ran at the **Morgan Library and Museum (55)** at 225 Madison Avenue. In April 2008, Dylan was awarded a Pulitzer Prize Special Citation, one of only three American musicians to be so honored (the others are Thelonious Monk and John Coltrane). *Together through Life* debuted at number one when it was released in April 2009. Most of the songs were co-written with Grateful Dead lyricist Robert Hunter, the first album since *Desire* on which Dylan extensively collaborated with another artist.

In many ways, Bob Dylan continues to permeate modern culture. In 2010, he was named one of twelve recipients of the National Medal of Arts. An exhibition of his artwork went on sale at London's Halycon Gallery. The exhibit included about one hundred works, and another exhibition of his paintings went on display at the Statens Museum for Kunst in Copenhagen. "I just draw what's interesting to me, and then I paint it," he said. The handwritten lyrics of "The Times They Are A-Changin'" with a fragment of "North Country Blues" on the reverse side were sold at auction in December 2010 for a whopping $422,500.

Todd Haynes's 2007 film *I'm Not There*, in which six characters (the thin, wild mercury Bob; cowboy Bob; hobo Bob; born-again Bob; celebrity Bob; and poetic Bob) embody the many moods of Bob Dylan, prompted the *New Yorker* to publish a cartoon depicting two slacker types with guitars and an empty pizza carton accompanied by the caption, "If you could be any Bob Dylan you wanted to, which Bob Dylan would you be?" Three years later, the magazine published another Dylan-inspired cartoon in a takeoff of *Blonde on Blonde*'s "Memphis Blues Again": commuters on a busy subway train try to ignore a bespectacled Dylan wannabe busker ("You've got those Stuck-in-the-Subway-Listening-to-a-Guy-Massacre-Dylan Blues").[112]

There are courses on Dylan and symposiums on Dylan. The list of tributes to him goes on and on. He has inspired novels, from Don DeLillo's *Great Jones Street* (1973) to Brian Morton's *The Dylanist* (1991) to Jonathan Lethem's *The Fortress of Solitude* (2003). In 2016, he was awarded the Nobel Prize in Literature "for having created new poetic expressions within the great American song tradition." Not everyone was pleased with the decision, however. Some maintained that since he was a songwriter, his works should not be considered literature or poetry. As Richard Thomas notes in his book *Why Bob Dylan Matters*, Irish critic Edna Longley called the reward "a ridiculous decision, and an insult to real poets." But her opinion seemed to be in the minority. Dylan's Nobel acceptance speech—in which he riffs on his many influences from Buddy Holly and Lead Belly to *The Odyssey*, *Moby Dick* and *All Quiet on the Western Front*—was published by Simon & Schuster as a thirty-two-page hardcover collectible edition in 2017. As we all know, Dylan did not accept the award in person. In his absence, Patti Smith was asked to represent him at the ceremony in Stockholm and chose to sing "A Hard Rain's A-Gonna Fall," a song she had loved since she was a teenager and also a favorite of her late husband. She thought about her mother, who had bought Smith her first Dylan album when she, Smith, was "barely sixteen," as she recalled in an essay in the *New Yorker*. As is also known, as she sang the song in front of the Swedish royal family and the world, she stumbled. She did not forget the words. Rather, overwhelmed by a "case of nerves," she simply was "unable to draw them out." But when she did continue, the end result was a stunning performance made all the more masterful for its vulnerability. You can see for yourself on YouTube.

In 2019, Dylan introduced an upscale, handcrafted American whiskey, Heaven's Door (as in "Knockin' on Heaven's Door"), in celebration of the fiftieth anniversary of his album *Nashville Skyline*. Dylan's artwork appears on the Heaven's Door website (www.heavensdoor.com). (The Heaven's Door

"Is Dylan Literature?" Is Dylan a writer or "just" a songwriter? Are great song lyrics great poetry? Did he deserve the Nobel Prize for Literature? Questions, questions, questions. Either way, Dylan became the first songwriter to win the award and the first American since novelist Toni Morrison in 1993. *Author collection.*

Distillery and Center for the Arts in downtown Nashville, which is expected to include a whiskey library, a restaurant, and live performance venue, was originally scheduled to open in 2020 in a 160-year-old former church at 410 Elm Street. But due to the pandemic, the date was pushed back.) In December 2020, he sold his song catalogue to Universal Music for more than $300 million. Also in 2020, he released *Rough and Rowdy Ways*, which not only received critical acclaim, but it also became his first number-one *Billboard* hit. The album is anchored by "Murder Most Foul," which was released as a single in March 2020. The seventeen-minute song is about many things, including the Kennedy assassination and the 1921 Tulsa Race Massacre ("Take me back to Tulsa to the scene of the crime"). In May 2022, the Bob Dylan Center (www.bobdylancenter.com), which is dedicated to the study and appreciation of Dylan and his worldwide cultural significance, is scheduled to open in downtown Tulsa. The center will feature exhibits, public programming, performances, lectures and publications and will house the Bob Dylan Archive Collection of more than 100,000 items spanning Dylan's long career, including handwritten manuscripts, notebooks and correspondence; personal documents and effects; unreleased studio and concert recordings; and musical instruments. Both the Guthrie and Dylan centers are part of the Tulsa Arts District and near the Greenwood District, once known as Black Wall Street and, most famously, the scene of the Tulsa massacre. And in honor of his eightieth birthday, the Tulsa University Institute for Dylan Studies presented a three-day virtual symposium from May 22 to 24, 2021, on Dylan and his career.

"THIEF OF THOUGHTS"

Dylan first came to New York to meet his idol, Woody Guthrie. It didn't take long for him to transcend his mentors. He may have borrowed other people's words and filched other people's melodies, but he did so in order to create something entirely new and fresh. "Yes, I am a thief of thoughts," he admits in "11 Outlined Epitaphs," but not, "I pray, a stealer of souls."

Dylan followed in the tradition of the folk process, or what academics today call intertextuality; the process by which artists of various genres create and deepen new meaning through the creative reuse of existing texts (or images or sounds). To Dylan, it was all part of the musical tradition. The great bard of Scotland, Robert Burns, did it. So did Dylan's musical hero, Woody Guthrie. To Sean Wilentz, it is a "form of larceny that is as American as apple pie, and cherry, pumpkin, and plum pie, too." Everybody took things from everybody else and made it their own. Dylan was, as Pete Seeger had once described himself, a link in a chain.

New York provided the midwesterner with a platform, an inspiration, and gave Dylan the freedom to soak up the ideas that flourished around him, floating in the thick, smoke-filled air of Village coffeehouses amid the odor of stale coffee. Dylan could have reinvented himself anywhere. But he didn't go just *anywhere*. He went *somewhere*. He deliberately chose New York, because New York, more than any other city or town, was his point of reference while growing up in Minnesota.

Dylan chose New York because, as he told Robert Hilburn in 2004, "everything" came out of New York. "I listened to the Yankees games on the radio, and the Giants and the Dodgers. All the radio programs…and the record companies" and even something as basic and ubiquitous as "the NBC chimes…would be from New York.…It seemed," he concluded, "like New York was the capital of the world." [113] It was the right place at the right time. "There was nowhere else he could have gone to become Bob Dylan," echoes music critic Anthony DeCurtis. "It is hard to imagine

Decades after he arrived in New York, Dylan's visage continues to haunt the streets of Greenwich Village. *Photo by author.*

where else he could have gone given what his aspirations were."[114]

Dylan is part of a rich tradition: Manhattan beckons the outsiders, the nonconformists, the misfits from elsewhere who are unhappy, unsatisfied or just plain lost in their hometowns to join in the grand experiment of living and working in New York City.

Artists as dissimilar as painter Jackson Pollock and novelist Dawn Powell came to New York, because, for them, it was the only place for an artist to be. In New York, said Powell, "people with nothing behind them but their wits can be and do everything."[115] Generations of young men and women before and since Dylan's arrival on that snowy January day have descended on the Village to reinvent themselves.

"The first impulse of adolescence is to wish to be an orphan or an amnesiac," writes Anatole Broyard in his Greenwich Village memoir *Kafka Was the Rage*. "Nobody in the Village had a family. We were all sprung from our own brows, spontaneously generated the way flies were once thought to have originated."[116]

When alternative country rocker Steve Earle was growing up in Texas, he dreamed of going to the Village. The Village that he envisioned was Dylan's *Freewheelin'* Village: the image of Dylan and Rotolo walking arm and arm down that snowy New York street resonated with the Texas teenager—so much so that, in 2005, Earle and his then wife, the singer-songwriter Allison Moorer, not only moved to the Village but also settled into an apartment on the very same block as the one that appears in the iconic photograph. Earle even called his 2007 album *Washington Square Serenade*. The way Earle sees it, he was able to make a living doing what he does because of the Village and its inhabitants. The folk scene "happened only because there were these three groups—the folk-singers, the musicologists, and the writers—who happened to be living in this several-block radius. If that scene doesn't happen," he continues, "then rock and roll never becomes literature. It just stays pop."[117]

Many people in the Village were doing what Dylan was doing: scribbling in small notepads, jotting down ideas and random thoughts.[118] They wrote in the cafés, on benches in Washington Square Park and, when struck by a moment of inspiration, leaning against walls, scrawling their precious back-of-a-napkin thoughts down before they disappeared. Broyard describes these fleeting literary moments as "postcards to literature that we never mailed."

While Dylan spent time in many corners of Manhattan, the Village exerted an irrefutable pull, and he returned to it again and again. He liked that the Village was different from the rest of Manhattan. Whereas Manhattan above Fourteenth Street forms a structured grid pattern, the Village is amorphous, fluid, haphazard, its narrow streets going off at odd angles. It is easy to get lost in the Village, in more ways than one.

Dylan's Village consisted of a loose-knit community of musicians. It was the kind of place where bars didn't need to advertise; people knew where to find them. It had a dream-like quality about it that, for a time, promoted creativity over monetary gain. It had a long tradition of giving people an opportunity to be who they wanted to be.

If New York was a world unto itself, Greenwich Village was, to Dylan, the city's shimmering, mysterious and enigmatic core. "The city…showed no favoritism," he observes. "Everything was always new, always changing." [119] He savored its rich literary and cultural history and appreciated its tolerance of human foibles. Fellow singer and exile Mark Spoelstra, who hailed from California, recalled that Dylan was not intimidated by the city. Instead, he accepted it at face value and "just kind of took it for granted." The part of the city that intrigued him the most, though, was Greenwich Village. [120]

Greenwich Village was also Dylan's inspiration. When he came to New York, his identity was still forming. John Cohen, a founder of the New Lost City Ramblers, thought the early Dylan was a beguiling mix of Woody Guthrie, Charlie Chaplin and James Dean. Dylan met like-minded folk and forged an identity that he could hang on to and embellish in the Village. The music that he discovered at places like the Folklore Center, Dylan told Mikal Gilmore of *Rolling Stone*, "was impossible to get anywhere really, except in a nucleus of a major city." [121]

SHAPE-SHIFTER

Cities change. Over the decades since Dylan first made his name there, New York—Manhattan in particular—has grown wealthier and whiter as American-born whites began moving back into the cities that their parents and grandparents abandoned years before. In the 1990s, Mayor Rudolph Giuliani, before he became Trump's bulldog and subsequently the laughingstock of late-night comedians, adopted the so-called broken windows theory: by fixing little problems before they turn into big problems (literally fixing broken windows), authorities can alleviate vandalism and reduce crime. (Not everyone agreed with that theory.) Meanwhile, in the early 2000s, the influx of Wall Street hotshots and dot-com entrepreneurs fueled a real estate boom. The trend continued until the recession that began in September 2008 slowed the growth. Yet the New York today is far beyond the reach of many aspiring musicians, writers and artists.

Like cities, people change. Dylan has undergone many transformations, many of the significant ones in New York. New York, part symbol and part reality, was the city of Dylan's dreams, the city that allowed him to fully adopt the personas of "Bob Dylan" so much so that his alter ego, Robert Zimmerman, became unrecognizable, somehow a stranger even to himself. "I don't know *who* I am most of the time," he told David Gates of *Newsweek*. New York represented freedom; it allowed him to escape from his past in order to create a new present. "It was a great place for me to learn and to meet others who were on similar journeys," he said.[122]

The contemporary Dylan is a traveling musical salesman, like, says Alex Ross, "B.B. King or Ralph Stanley or Willie Nelson." He is always putting on a show in one form or another, a never-ending show that may be coming to a town near you. And, as a man of many parts, many voices and many faces, he always wears a mask. Dylan was—is—the ultimate shape-shifter and trickster, a fabulist of the first order, the king of the masquerade.[123]

As I write this, New York—and the rest of the world—is in the middle of a global pandemic. We don't know what kind of changes—whether permanent or temporary—the coronavirus will have on our collective lives. We wait and see and hope for the best.

Meanwhile, Dylan goes on, his work an ongoing story. He is a man who is both out of time and timeless, and thus, no one particular place could ever truly hold Bob Dylan down forever. What, after all, is Bob Dylan, the former Robert Zimmerman, but a midwestern boy—a midwestern prophet—who made a name for himself, who found his place, in the Big Apple and on the world stage? Like another one of his mentors, the equally elusive Walt Whitman, he contains multitudes and is in a constant state of transformation. No city, not even New York, is big enough.

And yet New York shaped Dylan like no other city or town. It was the place to be, and Bob Dylan had to be there, if only until it was again time to move on.

NOTES

Introduction

1. Bob Dylan, *Chronicles: Volume One* (New York: Simon & Schuster, 2004), 257.
2. Dylan, *Chronicles*, 77; chapter 1. According to Andy Greene in *Rolling Stone*, Dylan's Hibbing home, where the singer lived from 1948 to 1959, was bought by Bill Pagel in 2019 for $84,000. In 2001, he purchased Dylan's first home, in Duluth, for $82,000.

1. Looking for Woody

3. *No Direction Home: Bob Dylan* (DVD; directed by Martin Scorsese, 2005).
4. Ibid.
5. Patti Smith, *Just Kids* (New York: Ecco, 2010).
6. *No Direction Home.*
7. Dylan, *Chronicles*, 243–45.
8. Ibid., 10; Manny Roth was the uncle of Van Halen lead singer David Lee Roth. He died in 2014.
9. Dave Van Ronk with Elijah Wald, *The Mayor of MacDougal Street: A Memoir* (New York: Da Capo Press, 2005), 158.
10. Ibid., 16.
11. *No Direction Home.*

12. Bob Spitz, *Dylan: A Biography* (New York: W.W. Norton, 1991), 130.
13. Robbie Woliver, *Hoot! A 25-Year History of the Greenwich Village Music Scene* (New York: St. Martin's, 1986), 66.
14. This section draws on the following sources: David Hajdu, *Positively 4ᵗʰ Street: The Lives and Times of Joan Baez, Bob Dylan, Mimi Baez Fariña, and Richard Fariña* (New York: Farrar, Straus and Giroux, 2001); Tony Fletcher, *All Hopped Up and Ready to Go: Music from the Streets of New York, 1927–77* (New York: W.W. Norton, 2009); Anthony DeCurtis, interview with the author.
15. Van Ronk and Wald, *Mayor of MacDougal Street*, 147.
16. Bonnie Bremser, "Poets and Odd Fellows," in *Beat Down to Your Soul*, ed. Ann Charters (New York: Penguin, 2001), 27. The Gaslight closed in 1971.
17. Dylan, *Chronicles*, 47, 49.
18. Suze Rotolo, *A Freewheelin' Time: A Memoir of Greenwich Village in the Sixties* (New York: Broadway Books, 2008), 93.
19. Ibid., 91.
20. Dylan, *Chronicles*, 83. "People who…": Bruce Weber, "Liam Clancy, 74, Last of the Folk Group," *New York Times*, December 5, 2009.
21. Dylan, *Chronicles*, 18.
22. Hajdu, *Positively 4th Street*, 36. In 1973, Izzy Young closed the Folklore Center and moved to Stockholm, where he opened a Scandinavian version of it called the Folklore Centrum and became a significant figure in Sweden, in effect, writes Stephen Petrus and Ronald Cohen, "transplanting Village culture to Scandinavia." See Stephen Petrus and Ronald D. Cohen, *Folk City: New York and the American Folk Music Revival* (New York: Oxford University Press, 2015), 304. Young died in Stockholm in 2019 at the age of ninety. He was the subject of a 1989 documentary, *Izzy Young: Talking Folklore Center*. His columns from *Sing Out!* magazine and other articles were collected in *The Conscience of the Folk Revival: The Writings of Israel "Izzy" Young*, ed. Scott Barretta (Lanham, MD: Scarecrow Press, 2013).
23. Dylan, *Chronicles*, 18.
24. Woliver, *Hoot!*, 82.
25. Dylan, *Chronicles*, 27. "According to Rotolo…": *Freewheelin' Time*, 97.
26. Rotolo, *Freewheelin' Time*, 96; "In her memoir…": ibid., 110.
27. *No Direction Home*.

2. I Is Someone Else

28. Hajdu, *Positively 4ᵗʰ Street*, 77.
29. "Folk Singing: Sibyl with Guitar," *Time*, November 23, 1962. The uncredited *Time* cover story on Joan Baez was written by the renowned essayist John McPhee, who was a contributing editor at the magazine before moving to the *New Yorker* in 1963, where he became a staff writer two years later. "When a documentary…": *How Sweet the Sound* (American Masters/PBS Television, 2009).
30. Rotolo, *Freewheelin' Time*, 22.
31. *Chronicles*, 62, 64.
32. Robert Shelton, *No Direction Home: The Life and Times of Bob Dylan* (New York: Da Capo Press, 2003), 110–11. 29: "Dylan had dreams…": *Chronicles*, 15.
33. Tom Piazza, "Pure Roots: The Smithsonian Has Reawakened Folkways Records, a Peerless Repository of Our Native Music," *Atlantic* (April 1995): 30. "Dylan admired Asch…": Hajdu, *Positively 4ᵗʰ Street*, 87.
34. Dunstan Prial, *The Producer: John Hammond and the Soul of American Music* (New York: Farrar, Straus & Giroux, 2006), 222.
35. Dylan, *Chronicles*, 279.
36. Ibid., 5.
37. Ibid.
38. Louis Menand, "Bob on Bob: Dylan Talks," *New Yorker*, September 4, 2006, 129, 34; "The first year…": Dylan, *Chronicles*, 73.

3. I'll Know My Song Well Before I Start Singing

39. David King Dunaway and Molly Beer, S*inging Out: An Oral History of America's Folk Music Revivals* (New York: Oxford University Press, 2010), 54.
40. Ibid., 123.
41. Rotolo, *Freewheelin' Time*, 220.
42. Ibid., 216, 9.
43. Dylan, *Chronicles*, 222.
44. Ken Emerson, *Always Magic in the Air: The Bomp and Brilliance of the Brill Building Era* (New York: Viking, 2005), 197.
45. Dylan, *Chronicles*, 3.
46. Shelton, *No Direction Home*, 145, 146.

47. Michael Gray, *The Bob Dylan Encyclopedia* (New York: Continuum, 2008), 62.
48. Ibid., 63. Gray adds that, by the end of 2003, Dylan had performed "Blowin' in the Wind" 935 times.
49. Clinton Heylin, *Revolution in the Air: The Songs of Bob Dylan, 1957–1973* (Chicago: Chicago Review Press, 2009), 78. Brian Hinton, *Bob Dylan Complete Discography* (New York: Universe, 2006), 230.
50. Bob Dylan, liner notes, Peter, Paul and Mary, *In the Wind* (Warner Brothers, 1963).
51. Dylan, *Chronicles*, 56.
52. Rotolo, *Freewheelin' Time*, 88.
53. Heylin, *Revolution in the Air*, 96.
54. Ibid., 94.
55. Bob Dylan, liner notes, *The Freewheelin' Bob Dylan* (Columbia, 1963); Heylin, *Revolution in the Air*, 97–98. The criminally underrated filmmaker Howard Alk (1930–1982) was Dylan's friend and close collaborator on various projects. He was also the original cofounder, along with Bernard Sahlins and Paul Sills, of Chicago's famous Second City and worked with Sills at Albert Grossman's Gate of Horn folk club. He assisted on several of Dylan's films, including *Don't Look Back* (1967) as assistant director, *Eat the Document* (1972) as cinematographer and editor and *Renaldo and Clara* (1978) as cinematographer and editor. In early 1963, Alk partnered with Grossman to open the Bear. According to J.R. Jones, Alk promoted the opening of the club "by riding around town on a motorcycle wearing a bear costume." See J.R. Jones, "Alk of the Town," *Chicago Reader*, January 9, 2009, and Bernard Sahlins, *Days and Nights at the Second City: A Memoir* (Chicago: Ivan R. Dee, 2002).
56. Heylin, *Revolution in the Air*, 171.
57. "I Am My Words," *Newsweek*, November 4, 1963, 94–95.

4. Revolution in the Air

58. Shelton, *No Direction Home*, 57. "Between the Town Hall...": Dylan, *Chronicles*, 89.
59. Dylan, *Chronicles*, 84.
60. Ibid., 269–70.
61. See Nat Hentoff, "The Crackin', Shakin', Breakin' Sounds," in *Studio A: The Bob Dylan Reader*, ed. Benjamin Hedin (New York: W. W. Norton, 2004), 22–39.

62. Heylin, *Revolution in the Air,* 156.

63. "The Playboy Interview: Bob Dylan," *Playboy*, March 1978.

64. Spitz, *Dylan: A Biography.*

65. *No Direction Home.*

66. For an overview of the debacle and Dylan's follow-up letter to the ECLC, see "Bob Dylan and the NECLC," www.corliss-lamont.org/dylan.htm (accessed November 27, 2009). Although he wrote the opus-like "Murder Most Foul" on his 2020 album *Rough and Rowdy Ways*, Dylan has long had an interest in the Kennedy assassination, and the song itself in typical Dylanesque fashion is full of cultural allusions, from the Tulsa Race Massacre of 1921 to the Birdman of Alcatraz. But then again, Dylan has a history of name-checking in his lyrics, as Adrian Grafe notes, finding some "similarity" between his very long prose-poem "11 Outlined Epitaphs" in the liner notes of *The Times They Are A-Changin'* and the song.

67. Rotolo, *Freewheelin' Time*, 257.

68. Hentoff, "Crackin', Shakin', Breakin' Sounds."

69. Sean Wilentz, liner notes, *Bob Dylan Live 1964 Concert at Philharmonic Hall, The Bootleg Series Vol. 6* (Columbia, 2004), 49.

70. Robert Shelton, "Bob Dylan Shows New Maturity in Program of His Folk Songs," *New York Times*, 1964, in *Bob Dylan Live 1964 Concert at Philharmonic Hall.*

71. Rotolo, *Freewheelin' Time*, 275.

72. "A Letter from Bob Dylan," *Broadside*, January 20, 1964.

5. Mystery Tramps and Napoleons in Rags

73. Luc Sante, "I Is Someone Else," *New York Review of Books*, March 10, 2005, 35.

74. Anne Waldman, "Bob Dylan and the Beats: Magpie Poetics, and Investigation and Memoir," in *Highway 61 Revisited: Bob Dylan's Road from Minnesota to the World*, ed. Colleen J. Sheehy and Thomas Swiss (Minneapolis: University of Minnesota Press, 2009), 252.

75. Dan Wakefield, *New York in the 50s* (New York: St. Martin's Griffin, 1992), 187.

76. Hentoff, "The Crackin', Shakin', Breakin' Sounds."

77. Irwin Silber, "An Open Letter," *Sing Out!*, November 1964, 22–23.

78. Heylin, *Revolution in the Air*, 239, 241.

79. Ibid., 265.

80. Bob Dylan, liner notes, *The Freewheelin' Bob Dylan* (Columbia, 1963).
81. Greil Marcus, *Like a Rolling Stone: Bob Dylan at the Crossroads* (New York: Public Affairs, 2005), 137–38. In *Chronicles* (227), Dylan acknowledges his debt to the Brill Building composers and other composers of that era—Gerry Goffin and Carole King, Barry Mann and Cynthia Weil, Doc Pomus and Mort Shuman, Jerry Leiber and Mike Stoller and Neil Sedaka—as "the songwriting masters of the Western world."
82. Heylin, *Revolution in the Air*, 274.
83. Gray, *Bob Dylan Encyclopedia*, 613.
84. Shelton, *No Direction Home*, 236.

6. Madness, Madness Everywhere

85. Sid Griffin, *Million Dollar Bash: Bob Dylan, the Band, and the Basement Tapes* (London: Jawbone Press, 2007).
86. *No Direction Home.*
87. Dylan, *Chronicles*, 113.
88. Terry Teachout, "Stuck Inside the Theater with the Broadway Blues Again," *Wall Street Journal*, October 27, 2006.
89. Twyla Tharp, quoted in Gia Kourlas, "Tharp Is Back Where the Air Is Rarefied," *New York Times*, March 5, 2010.
90. Dylan, *Chronicles*, 117.
91. "Interview with Kurt Loder, *Rolling Stone*, June 21, 1984," in *Bob Dylan: The Essential Interviews*, ed. Jonathan Cott (New York: Wenner, 2006), 301. The second, less famous, Woodstock Festival took place on August 12–14, 1994, at Winston Farm, in Saugerties, at the site that was proposed for the first Woodstock. More than 300,000 people attended what Barney Hoskyns calls a "mass mud bath." In addition to Dylan, performers included The Band, John Sebastian, Santana, Todd Rundgren, Crosby, Stills & Nash and Joe Cocker as well as Metallica, Green Day, Nine Inch Nails, Red Hot Chili Peppers, Traffic, Aerosmith, the Allman Brothers and Peter Gabriel. Among the songs that Dylan sang were "All Along the Watchtower" and "I Shall Be Released," both with Woodstock links. See Barney Hoskyns, *Small Town Talk* (Boston: Da Capo Press, 2016), 333.
92. Dylan, *Chronicles*, 118.
93. "Interview with Ron Rosenbaum, *Playboy*, March 1978," in Cott, *The Essential Interviews*, 211.

94. "Interview with Kurt Loder."

95. Dylan, *Chronicles*, 131.

96. Greil Marcus, "Self Portrait No. 25" in *Studio A: The Bob Dylan Reader*, ed. Benjamin Hedin (New York: W.W. Norton, 2004), 74; it originally appeared in the July 23, 1970 issue of *Rolling Stone*.

97. Howard Sounes, *Down the Highway: The Life of Bob Dylan* (New York: Grove Press, 2001).

98. Bert Cartwright, "The Mysterious Norman Raeben," web.archive.org/web/20011007203741/http://www.geoci-   ties.com/Athens/266 (accessed November 27, 2009).

99. Ibid.

7. Something Like a Circus

100. Shelton, *No Direction Home*, 447.

101. Paul Colby, "Bob Dylan: The King and His Court," in *The Greenwich Village Reader: Fiction, Poetry, and Reminiscences, 1872–2002*, ed. June Skinner Sawyers (New York: Cooper Square Press/Rowman & Littlefield, 2001), 685.

102. Sounes, *Down the Highway*, 293.

103. Woliver, *Hoot!*, 169. The Rolling Thunder Revue took its name from the code name Operation Rolling Thunder, which referred to the bombing campaign in North Vietnam from March 1965 to October 1968 during the Vietnam War.

104. Clinton Heylin, *Bob Dylan: Behind the Shades Revisited* (New York: William Morrow, 2001), 491.

105. Bruce Springsteen, "The Rock and Roll Hall of Fame Speech," in Hedin, *Bob Dylan Reader*, 203.

106. Bob Dylan Rock and Roll Hall of Fame acceptance speech. See rockhall.com/inductees/bsh-dylan.

107. When analyzing the songs of *Planet Waves*, John Hinchey refers to "the history we carry around with us." Quoted in David Pichaske, *Song of the North Country: A Midwest Framework to the Songs of Bob Dylan* (New York: Continuum, 2010), 188.

108. Clinton Heylin, *Still on the Road: The Songs of Bob Dylan, 1974–2000* (Chicago: Chicago Review Press, 2010), 426.

109. Roger Friedman, "Bob Dylan Celebrates New York," *Fox News*, November 20, 2001.

110. Peter Edidin, "Dylanologists Check Which Way the Wind Blows," *New York Times*, May 7, 2005.

8. I Am Many

111. David Gates, "The Book of Bob," *Newsweek*, October 4, 2004.

112. *New Yorker*, December 10, 2007; *New Yorker*, October 25, 2010.

113. "Interview with Robert Hilburn, *Los Angeles Times*, April 4, 2004," in Cott, *Essential Interviews*, 434.

114. Anthony DeCurtis, interview with the author.

115. Shaun O'Connell, *Remarkable, Unspeakable New York: A Literary History* (Boston: Beacon Press, 1997), 268.

116. Anatole Broyard, *Kafka Was the Rage: A Greenwich Village Memoir* (New York: Vintage Books, 1997), 29.

117. John Seabrook, "Takes a Village Dept.: Transplant," *New Yorker*, June 11, 2007.

118. Broyard, *Kafka Was the Rage*, 70.

119. Dylan, *Chronicles*, 103

120. Spitz, *Dylan: A Biography*, 664.

121. Interview with Mikal Gilmore, *Rolling Stone*, December 22, 2001," in Cott, *Essential Interviews*, 424.

122. Gates, "Book of Bob."

123. Alex Ross, *Listen to This* (New York: Farrar, Straus & Giroux, 2010), 287.

FURTHER READING

Bartholomew, Rafe. *Two and Two: McSorley's, My Dad, and Me*. New York: Little, Brown, 2017.

Beard, Rick, and Leslie Cohen Berlowitz, eds. *Greenwich Village: Culture and Counterculture*. Brunswick, NJ: Published for the Museum of New York by Rutgers University Press, 1991.

Bell, Ian. *Once Upon a Time: The Lives of Bob Dylan*. New York: Pegasus, 2013.

————. *Time Out of Mind: The Lives of Bob Dylan*. New York: Pegasus, 2014.

Brinkley, Douglas. "Still Painting His Masterpieces." *New York Times*, June 14, 2020.

Broyard, Anatole. *Kafka Was the Rage: A Greenwich Village Memoir*. New York: Vintage Books, 1997.

Chandler, Kurt. "Poetry in Motion: Tracing Bob Dylan's Minnesota Roots." *Chicago Tribune*, November 21, 2016.

Charters, Ann, ed. *Beat Down to Your Soul: What Was the Beat Generation?* New York: Penguin, 2001.

Cohen, Ronald D. *Rainbow Quest: The Folk Revival & American Society, 1940–1970*. Amherst: University of Massachusetts Press, 2002.

Cott, Jonathan, ed. *Bob Dylan: The Essential Interviews*. New York: Wenner, 2006.

Dettmar, Kevin J.H., ed. *The Cambridge Companion to Bob Dylan*. Cambridge: Cambridge University Press, 2009.

Dunaway, David King, and Molly Beer. *Singing Out: An Oral History of America's Folk Music Revivals*. New York: Oxford University Press, 2010.

Dylan, Bob. *Chronicles: Volume One.* New York: Simon & Schuster, 2004.
———. *The Nobel Lecture.* New York: Simon & Schuster, 2017.
Emerson, Ken. *Always Music in the Air: The Bomp and Brilliance of the Brill Building Era.* New York: Viking, 2005.
Fletcher, Tony. *All Hopped Up and Ready to Go: Music from the Streets of New York, 1927–77.* New York: W.W. Norton, 2009.
Grafe, Adrian. "Time Out of Joint." *Times Literary Supplement,* May 15, 2020.
Gray, Michael. *The Bob Dylan Encyclopedia.* New York: Continuum, 2008.
———. *Hand Me My Travelin' Shoes: In Search of Blind Willie McTell.* London: Bloomsbury, 2008.
———. *Song & Dance Man III: The Art of Bob Dylan.* London: Continuum, 2000.
Greene, Andy, "Bob Dylan Super-Fan Purchases Singer's Childhood Home in Hibbing, Minnesota." *Rolling Stone,* July 12, 2019.
Griffin, Sid. *Million Dollar Bash: Bob Dylan, the Band, and the Basement Tapes.* London: Jawbone Press, 2007.
Hajdu, David. *Positively 4th Street: The Lives and Times of Joan Baez, Bob Dylan, Mimi Baez Fariña, and Richard Fariña.* New York: Farrar, Straus & Giroux, 2001.
Hamilton, Ed. *Legends of the Chelsea Hotel: Living with Artists and Outlaws at New York's Rebel Mecca.* New York: Thunder's Mouth Press, 2007.
Hedin, Benjamin, ed. *Studio A: The Bob Dylan Reader.* New York: W.W. Norton, 2004.
Heylin, Clinton. *Bob Dylan: Behind the Shades Revisited.* New York: William Morrow, 2001.
———. *Revolution in the Air: The Songs of Bob Dylan, 1957–1973.* Chicago: Chicago Review Press, 2009.
———. *Still on the Road: The Songs of Bob Dylan, 1974–2000.* Chicago: Chicago Review Press, 2010.
Hinton, Brian. *Bob Dylan Complete Discography.* New York: Universe, 2006.
Hoskyns, Barney. *Small Town Talk: Bob Dylan, the Band, Van Morrison, Janis Joplin, Jimi Hendrix & Friends in the Wilds of Woodstock.* Boston: Da Capo Press, 2016.
Inside Llewyn Davis (2013). Press kit. www.insidellewyndavis.com. Articles include "The Coen Brothers' Real Deal" by Robert Christgau; "Before the Flood: Llewyn Davis, Dave Van Ronk, and the Village Folk Scene of 1961" by Elijah Wald; "Daft Folk" by John Jeremiah Sullivan; "'That'll Never Happen No More'" by Sean Wilentz; and "Llewyn Davis, the Guitar, and the Democratization of American Music" by David Hajdu.

Kinney, David. *The Dylanologists: Adventures in the Land of Bob*. New York: Simon & Schuster, 2014.

Kraker, Dan. "Bob Dylan's Hometown of Hibbing Struggles How to Honor Its Most Famous Son." Minnesota Public Radio (MPR) News, December 9, 2016.

Latham, Sean, ed. *The World of Bob Dylan*. Cambridge: Cambridge University Press, 2021.

Marcus, Greil. *Invisible Republic: Bob Dylan's Basement Tapes*. New York: Owl Books/Henry Holt, 1998.

———. *Like a Rolling Stone: Bob Dylan at the Crossroads*. New York: Public Affairs, 2005.

Maymudes, Victor, and Jacob Maymudes. *Another Side of Bob Dylan: A Personal History on the Road and off the Tracks*. New York: St. Martin's Press, 2014.

McCarron, Andrew. *Light Come Shining: The Transformations of Bob Dylan*. New York: Oxford University Press, 2017.

McLeod, Kembrew. *The Downtown Pop Underground*. New York: Abrams Press, 2018.

Mitchell, Joseph. *Up in the Old Hotel and Other Stories*. New York: Vintage, 1993.

Moss, Jeremiah. *Vanishing New York: How a Great City Lost Its Soul*. New York: Dey Street/William Morrow, 2017.

O'Connell, Shaun. *Remarkable, Unspeakable New York: A Literary History*. Boston: Beacon Press, 1997.

Perchuk, Andrew, and Rani Singh, eds. *Harry Smith: The Avant-Garde in the American Vernacular*. Los Angeles: Getty Research Institute 2010.

Petrus, Stephen, and Ronald D. Cohen. *Folk City: New York and the American Folk Music Revival*. Foreword by Peter Yarrow. New York: Oxford University Press, 2015.

Pichaske, David. *Song of the North Country: A Midwest Framework to the Songs of Bob Dylan*. New York: Continuum, 2010.

Prial, Dustin. *The Producer: John Hammond and the Soul of American Music*. New York: Farrar, Straus & Giroux, 2006.

Ricks, Christopher. *Dylan's Visions of Sin*. New York: Ecco, 2003.

Ross, Alex. *Listen to This*. New York: Farrar, Straus & Giroux, 2010.

Rotolo, Suze. *A Freewheelin' Time: A Memoir of Greenwich Village in the Sixties*. New York: Broadway Books, 2008.

Sawyers, June Skinner, ed. *The Best in Rock Fiction*. Anthony DeCurtis, guest editor. New York: Hal Leonard, 2005.

———. *The Greenwich Village Reader: Fiction, Poetry, and Reminiscences, 1872–2002*. New York: Cooper Square Press/Rowman & Littlefield, 2001.

Sheehy, Colleen J., and Thomas Swiss, eds. *Highway 61 Revisited: Bob Dylan's Road from Minnesota to the World*. Minneapolis: University of Minnesota Press, 2009.

Shelton, Robert. *No Direction Home: The Life and Times of Bob Dylan*. New York: Da Capo Press, 2003.

Smith, Caspar Llewellyn. "Flash-back: Bob Dylan." *Guardian*, September 18, 2005.

Smith, Patti. "How Does It Feel." *New Yorker*, December 14, 2016.

———. *Just Kids*. New York: Ecco, 2010.

———. *M Train*. New York: Alfred A. Knopf, 2015.

Snyder, Robert W. *The Voice of the City: Vaudeville and Popular Culture in New York*. Chicago: Ivan R. Dee, 2000.

Sorel, Edward. *The Mural at the Waverly Inn: A Portrait of Greenwich Village Bohemians*. Text by Dorothy Gallagher. Introduction by Graydon Carter. New York: Pantheon Books, 2008.

Sounes, Howard. *Down the Highway: The Life of Bob Dylan*. New York: Grove Press, 2001.

Spitz, Bob. *Dylan: A Biography*. New York: W.W. Norton, 1991.

Strausbaugh, John. *The Village: 400 Years of a History of Beats and Bohemians, Radicals and Rogues: A History of Greenwich Village*. New York: Ecco, 2013.

Thomas, Richard F. *Why Bob Dylan Matters*. New York: Dey Street/William Morrow, 2017.

Tippins, Sherill. *Inside the Dream Palace: The Life and Times of New York's Legendary Chelsea Hotel*. New York: Houghton Mifflin Harcourt, 2013.

Van Ronk, Dave with Elijah Ward. *The Mayor of MacDougal Street: A Memoir*. New York: Da Capo Press, 2005.

Vincentelli, Elisabeth. "Bob Dylan Found Them: 'Girl from the North Country' Cast Members Talk about the First Time They Heard His Music." *New York Times*, March 1, 2020.

Wakefield, Dan. *New York in the 50s*. New York: St. Martin's Griffin, 1992.

Wetzsteon, Ross. *Republic of Dreams Greenwich Village: The American Bohemia, 1910–1960*. New York: Simon & Schuster, 2002.

Wilentz, Sean. *Bob Dylan in America*. New York: Doubleday, 2010.

Woliver, Robbie. *Hoot! A 25-Year History of the Greenwich Village Music Scene*. New York: St. Martin's Press, 1986.

Young, Rob. *Electric Eden: Unearthing Britain's Visionary Music*. New York: Faber and Faber, 2010.

ABOUT THE AUTHOR

Photo by Theresa Albini.

orn in Glasgow, Scotland, June Skinner Sawyers has written or edited more than twenty books, many with a music or literary theme, including *Long Walk Home: Reflections on Bruce Springsteen*; *Cabaret FAQ: All That's Left to Know About the Broadway and Cinema Classic*; *Celtic Music: A Complete Guide*; *Tougher Than the Rest: 100 Best Bruce Springsteen Songs*; *Read the Beatles*; *Racing in the Street: The Bruce Springsteen Reader*; *The Best in Rock Fiction*; and *The Greenwich Village Reader*. Her work has appeared in the *Chicago Tribune, San Francisco Chronicle, Sing Out!, Dirty Linen, Booklist*, the *Common Review*, the *Times Literary Review* and the *Third Coast Review*. She has taught courses on Bob Dylan and the American song tradition at the Newberry Library in Chicago.

Visit us at
www.historypress.com